Bigger Than Bitcoin

Secret Wealth Strategies of the 4th Industrial Revolution

Worldwide Worthy

Bigger Than Bitcoin LLC

I dedicate this book to my son, whose passion ignited this journey and whose bravery continues to inspire me, and to my daughter, whose laughter and strength remind me to never stop growing. To my parents, especially my mother, for never giving up on me; for that, this book is for you.

And to all the dreamers, innovators, and risk-takers who dare to imagine a better future. Thank you for the inspiration, motivation, and belief that anything is possible

CONTENTS

Title Page

Copyright

Dedication

Preface

Introduction: 1

Chapter 1 4

Chapter 2 7

Chapter 3 10

Chapter 4 13

Chapter 5 15

Chapter 6 17

Chapter 7 19

Chapter 8 21

Chapter 9 22

Chapter 10 24

Chapter 11 26

Chapter 12 30

Chapter 13 32

Chapter 14   42

Chapter 15   49

Chapter 16   56

Chapter 17   79

Chapter 18   86

Chapter 19   92

Chapter 20   98

Chapter 21   104

Chapter 22   110

Chapter 23   119

Epilogue   131

Acknowledgement   133

About The Author   135

PREFACE

Welcome, and thank you for embarking on this transformative journey with Bigger Than Bitcoin: Secret Wealth Strategies of the 4th Industrial Revolution.

This book represents far more than words on a page—it's a roadmap for navigating one of the most pivotal shifts in human history. As we stand on the cusp of the 4th Industrial Revolution, the world as we know it is being rewritten. Blockchain, artificial intelligence, quantum computing, and other groundbreaking technologies are reshaping economies, industries, and the very way we live and work. Change is inevitable, but thriving within it requires insight, strategy, and action.

I created Bigger Than Bitcoin to empower individuals like you—forward-thinkers who recognize the power of this moment and are ready to seize the immense opportunities it brings. This book is your first step into a world where knowledge, strategy, and bold action can transform your life. By diving into these pages, you're joining a movement aimed at creating a new generation of millionaires and billionaires equipped to lead and innovate in this revolutionary era.

This journey is not just about building personal wealth; it's about something greater—empowering others, creating lasting impact, and redefining what's possible. By understanding and applying the principles and strategies in this book, you're not just participating in change—you're helping to shape the future.

The path ahead is filled with challenges, but it's also brimming with unparalleled opportunities. Bigger Than Bitcoin is here to equip you with the tools and knowledge to thrive, not just survive, in the financial revolution that's unfolding.

This is more than a book—it's a movement, a manifesto, and a mission. The future is unwritten, and I'm excited to see how you will contribute to it. Together, we're building the next era of wealth and prosperity.

Let's get started,
Dan Worldwide Worthy

INTRODUCTION:

UNLOCKING THE FUTURE OF WEALTH: EMBRACE THE 4TH INDUSTRIAL REVOLUTION

Welcome to a journey that will reshape how you think about wealth, technology, and the future. This book is your gateway to understanding and investing in the rapidly evolving crypto and blockchain space—an essential step to positioning yourself at the forefront of the 4th Industrial Revolution (4IR). Whether you're a newcomer to cryptocurrency or already familiar with its basics, there has never been a better time to deepen your knowledge and discover the immense opportunities lying ahead. The digital landscape is rapidly changing, and those who act now will reap the rewards in the future.

The future is full of opportunities and potential, and it's all thanks to the revolutionary technology of blockchain and cryptocurrencies. It's not just a passing trend or fad, but rather a transformative force that is set to disrupt and reshape industries across the globe. Blockchain technology, like the internet, has the potential to connect the world in previously unimaginable ways by decentralizing power and revolutionizing the creation, transfer, and security of value. However, this transformation extends beyond the financial sector. It could affect everything from how we work and interact to how we own and control our data.

Blockchain is at the heart of the 4th Industrial Revolution in this era. And the best part? You still have the opportunity to engage and contribute to this significant change. No matter your age or background, now is the perfect time to jump in and actively participate in this global transformation. Don't let the fear of missing out hold you back—there are still plenty of opportunities to generate wealth in this space. But as with any emerging industry, these opportunities won't last forever. So, if you want to unlock the future of wealth and be a part of shaping the world to come; the time to act is now. Don't let this chance pass by.

In this book, I'll guide you through strategies for building wealth during the 4IR. You'll learn how to evaluate blockchain projects, understand the long-term potential of cryptocurrencies, and make informed decisions to position yourself for success. More than just financial gain, this journey is about empowering yourself with knowledge, educating others, and sharing insights to succeed in this new era. We are all part of this seismic global shift.

We are living in an age of monumental change, one that brings with it an unprecedented opportunity for those willing to educate themselves and invest wisely. The world is moving toward decentralization, digital assets, and new forms of wealth. Now is your chance to enter on the ground floor. This is your call to action: educate yourself, spread the knowledge and shape the future. The world of tomorrow is being built today, and your role in it starts right now.

Don't let these tokens go unspoken. It's time to stake your claim.

CHAPTER 1

The Bitcoin Pizza Story: A Slice of History

The Moment That Sparked a Global Revolution

If you're like most people, the first time you heard about

Bitcoin[1] was around 2009—a mysterious new form of digital "currency" that few could grasp. Back then, it was widely dismissed as either a scam or a fleeting internet experiment. The price? A laughable $0.00099 per Bitcoin.

Fast forward to May 22, 2010, when a programmer named Laszlo Hanyecz paid 10,000 Bitcoins for two Papa John's pizzas from Jeremy Sturdivant. The value of Bitcoin was a modest $41 at that time. While this transaction seemed insignificant, it would go on to be immortalized as the first commercial Bitcoin transaction in history.

Fourteen years later, Bitcoin soared to an all-time high of over $90,000 per coin. Making those two pizzas worth an astonishing $900 million—or approximately $56.25 million per slice. The significance of this moment can't be overstated, as it marked Bitcoin's evolution from an obscure digital asset to a mainstream phenomenon.

When Bitcoin reached its all-time high, it wasn't just about the value of the currency. It was about the validation and recognition of the entire cryptocurrency market. Suddenly, people who had dismissed Bitcoin as a fad were forced to take notice. The rise in value, which was unprecedented, sparked a frenzy of investment and speculation, leading to even more growth in the market. It was a turning point for the industry and solidified Bitcoin's place as a legitimate and valuable asset. But beyond the financial implications, Bitcoin's success also had a significant impact on the technology world.

The underlying blockchain technology that powers Bitcoin has the potential to revolutionize industries beyond just finance. From supply chain management to healthcare, the possibilities are endless. The rise of Bitcoin also brought attention to the importance of decentralization and the potential for a more equitable distribution of wealth. It opened up a whole new world of possibilities and sparked a global conversation about the future of money and technology.

Today, Bitcoin continues to evolve and gain mainstream acceptance, with more and more companies and institutions adopting it as a form of payment. Its impact on the world of finance and technology cannot be overstated, and its journey from two pizzas to a $900 million valuation will be remembered as a pivotal moment in history. As we continue to explore the potential of cryptocurrency and blockchain technology, the sky's the limit for what the future may hold.

My own journey into the world of crypto started in a way familiar to many—hearing rumors, entertaining the idea, but not fully grasping its potential. I didn't dive in immediately. But as fate would have it, my son introduced me to the crypto space in a way that I couldn't ignore, setting me on the path toward what would become a life-changing discovery.

As Bitcoin continues to redefine wealth and technology, my objective is to help others embark on the same journey—because it is not too late. The future is still being written, and you can be a part of it.

CHAPTER 2

A Father First: Navigating New Worlds While Facing Old Battles

How a Father's Love Led to Bitcoin and a Lifelong Lesson

In October 2015, my son, a high school sophomore, moved back to Brooklyn with his mother. New York City was a completely different world compared to the quiet suburban life he'd known in Maryland. Like many teenagers, he veered off course and became entangled with some negative influences. His new friends had introduced him to an illegal game of "free shopping," or, as some New Yorkers would say, "clapping," in which pricey packages—ranging from designer clothing to technological gadgets—arrived at delivery places without any payment.

One day, his mother discovered some of these packages. Suspicious about where they came from—especially for a teenager with no income—she called me, furious and deeply worried. I could hear the fear and frustration in her voice, and while I tried to stay calm, I was boiling inside. My son had always promised me he'd protect his mother and keep trouble far from her. Now, we were facing a situation neither of us wanted.

I told her I'd handle it and immediately drove from Maryland to Brooklyn that night. I slept in my car outside their building, just waiting. The next morning, when my son stepped out, he didn't see me coming. The streets had taught me many lessons, and while I wasn't proud of it, I knew how to handle situations like these. I wasn't going to let my son go down a path that would destroy him. He needed to understand that his actions carried consequences—life wasn't a game.

After our confrontation, I calmed down and realized that more than anything, my son needed protection and guidance. I brought him back to Maryland for the weekend, determined to figure out what was really going on. As we talked, it became clear that he didn't fully grasp the seriousness of his actions.

"It's just internet money, Dad," he explained casually. "You can't even hold it, but you can buy stuff with it. It's not that serious. Everyone's doing it." I was frustrated but also intrigued. "Internet money? What are you talking about?" That's when he mentioned the word that would change my life: Bitcoin.

At that time, I had no idea what Bitcoin was. I pulled out my phone and started searching. I quickly learned it was a digital currency based on something called **blockchain technology**[2]. The more I read, the more fascinated I became. I didn't fully understand it then, but I knew I had stumbled onto something significant. I had to learn more. I asked my son where he got his Bitcoins, and he explained that he used Bitcoin **ATMs**[3], where you could exchange cash for digital coins. "Show me," I said.

That night, we found ourselves at a gas station just outside South Baltimore, standing in front of a Bitcoin ATM. For a couple hundred dollars, I bought two Bitcoins. At the time, it didn't seem like much, but that moment made Bitcoin real for me. The next day, during our drive back to Brooklyn, I had a long talk with my son. I warned him to stay out of trouble but also admitted that maybe, just maybe, we should hold on to those Bitcoins and see what happened. I had no idea then that this spur-of-the-moment decision, born out of curiosity and concern for my son, would end up changing our lives forever.

CHAPTER 3

We Fall to Get Back Up: The Accidental Windfall

How a Casual Investment Led to an Unexpected Fortune
In early 2017, my coworker Sean walked into my office with excitement in his voice. "Did you see Bitcoin hit $1,000?" he asked, reminding me of the Bitcoins I had purchased with my son in 2015. I was shocked by the price jump and annoyed that I hadn't bought more. It was tax season, and we decided to invest some of our returns into Bitcoin. I even dipped into my savings, reasoning that if it had quadrupled in less than two years, who knew where it could go in the next five to ten years?

Around that time, my cousin went through a rough breakup and needed a place to stay. Without a second thought, I offered him my spare bedroom. I was working at BWI Airport then, so I even helped him land a job there. Life wasn't much easier for my coworker, Butter. His marriage was falling apart, and he was battling depression. Seeing him struggle, I opened my home to him too, offering a spot on the couch. It's amusing how life brings people together, especially in difficult times. Whatever we needed—a place to crash or just some simple understanding—we found it in each other.

A few months later, my lease was up, and with both of them living with me, I decided to move into a bigger place.

I figured it would give everyone space to get back on their feet. Little did I know, this was just the beginning of the chaos. Soon after, a friend from Arizona reached out. He had lost his job and apartment and was living in shelters. He asked for money, but instead, I offered him a job at the airport if he came to Maryland. He joined the growing crew at my house, which now felt like a full house with different work shifts—7 AM to 3 PM, 3 PM to 11 PM, and 11 PM to 7 AM. Somehow, it all seemed manageable.

Then my cousins were kicked out of their mother's house in Jersey. They showed up at my door, and now two more bodies were added to our already crowded home. I didn't mind, though, as things between me and my daughter's mother, Sophie, were looking up. We had plans to move back in together in the fall, which seemed like the perfect solution. But life had other plans.

By the summer, my son had graduated high school but wasn't sure about his next steps. We considered the military, but given his love for substances the military frowned upon, we leaned toward college. The problem was, with his late application, there were no on-campus housing options. He would be forced to stay at home, but our house was already overflowing.

As if things couldn't get more stressful, my job at Baltimore Washington International Airport ended. For the first time in years, I found myself unemployed. In November, I threw myself into entrepreneurial ventures, reselling limited-edition Starbucks items and rare M&Ms. The whole household pitched in, and for a while, business was booming. But just as quickly as it grew, it slowed, leaving us with piles of unsold inventory. I had invested the majority of my savings in this venture, and now we found ourselves in a precarious situation.

To make matters worse, my son was slipping into his own struggles. He spent his days smoking weed and barely putting effort into his college courses. I tried banning him from parties until his grades improved, but at 18, he saw himself as an adult. One weekend, my cousin invited him to a party, and I reluctantly agreed, even though my gut told me not to. That night, I received the call that every parent fears—my son had sustained a stab wound. My cousin's frantic voice explained what had happened, and without hesitation, I jumped in my car and sped to the scene. My son was bleeding, slipping in and out of consciousness. I didn't know if he would make it.

The knife had come dangerously close to his heart, and as I drove, all I could think about was how I had failed him. He kept mumbling apologies, pleading with me to tell his mother he loved her if he didn't make it. Desperate to keep him focused, I slapped him hard. "You're not dying," I said firmly. "You're just cold because the windows are down." We made it to the hospital just in time. After 45 stitches, the doctors assured me he'd recover physically. But the emotional scars on both of us would take much longer to heal. In that moment, I couldn't shake the feeling that karma was finally catching up to me. Not by hitting me directly, but by hurting the one person I loved most. I had lived through so much, but now I feared my past was casting its shadow on my son.

CHAPTER 4

From a Black Friday to a Crypto Christmas

How a Bitcoin Surge Saved Christmas

I endured some of the worst weeks of my life following that harrowing night with my son. I was already struggling to process the fear and guilt, but things only got more complicated when more family members started showing up at my door, each in need of a place to stay.

I'd always been the one people relied on during tough times, but with seven people packed into a small three-bedroom apartment, no job, and the holidays fast approaching, I felt like I was suffocating. We managed to scrape together a small Thanksgiving meal, but Christmas was looming, and I had no money for gifts—normally I did all my shopping on Black Friday. By that Friday, it felt like everything was unraveling, and I had no idea how to put the pieces back together.

Then, amidst all the chaos, something unexpected happened. A notification popped up on my phone: "A **sell limit order**[4] has been executed.". At first, I didn't know what it meant. I hadn't been trading anything, and I hadn't been keeping track of the markets. Then, another alert followed, showing a deposit in my account—an amount so large, I could hardly believe it. For a moment, I thought it had to be a mistake.

Then it hit me: months earlier, I had set a sell limit order for my Bitcoin at $20,000, and it had just been triggered. The price had skyrocketed, and the proceeds were sitting in my account. It was December 15, 2017, and Bitcoin had hit $20,000 per coin. My automatic sell order had gone through, and over $200,000 was now in my account.

In that moment, everything changed. That single sell order saved Christmas—and, honestly, saved us from financial collapse. I cashed out, and for the first time, my family felt the true impact of Bitcoin. What could have been the coldest Christmas of our lives became our first "Crypto Christmas," a holiday filled with relief, gratitude, and amazement at how quickly our fortunes had turned.

Looking back, that moment solidified my belief in the power of cryptocurrency. It wasn't just about the money; it was about the possibilities. Bitcoin had rescued us in a way I never could have imagined, and I knew from that day on that this technology was bigger than any of us could fully understand. From that point forward, I was committed to learning everything I could about it—and sharing what I learned with others.

CHAPTER 5

A New Start: The Pivot from Crypto to Business Ventures

Returning to Business While Keeping an Eye on Crypto
I'd love to tell you that after making over $200,000 from Bitcoin, I became a crypto expert, trading like a Wall Street professional and growing my fortune. But that's not how things played out. To be honest, I didn't view that money as a result of any skill or strategy—it felt like pure luck. I hadn't been following the markets closely, and if I had, I probably would've cashed out much earlier. The whole thing felt surreal.

What really puzzled me was how my sell order had even been triggered. Bitcoin's all-time high at that point had been $19,783.21 on December 17th, yet my sell order at $20,000 had gone through. That's when I learned about a **bid-ask spread**[5].

In simple terms, the bid-ask spread is the difference between what buyers are willing to pay (the bid) and what sellers are asking for (the ask). My sell order had been triggered because someone was willing to buy at a slightly higher price than the official listing. Understanding this opened my eyes to how much more there was to cryptocurrency markets than just watching prices fluctuate. It was a marketplace with its dynamics, and mastering those dynamics would be critical if I wanted to succeed in the future.

I was hesitant to jump into the world of cryptocurrency right away, even with my newfound understanding. Instead, I turned my focus back to my successful business ventures. With the value of Bitcoin dropping, I wasn't fully confident in my knowledge of the crypto market. So, I decided to put my energy into scaling the businesses I had already built. My resale business was thriving, and I started exploring new opportunities, like starting a **CBD**[6] company with an ex-girlfriend who wanted to partner with me on a dispensary project in Los Angeles.

My used clothing business took off like never before. In just six months, we went from operating out of a small storage unit with only 800 items to processing over 30,000 pieces in a larger warehouse in Baltimore. Our success was unprecedented, with one of my eBay stores skyrocketing from a limit of 200 items to over 60,000. My family and I were sourcing over 1,000 units a day from all over the country, with our most valuable finds coming from the Goodwill warehouse in Queens, New York. It was a whirlwind of growth and success, and I was grateful for the opportunity to expand my business ventures.

CHAPTER 6

The Source: From a Storage Unit to an Empire

The Beginnings of a Thriving Resale Business
Let me take you back to where it all began. In the fall of 2017, a close friend needed my help. She asked for a ride to the post office and needed some assistance at her storage unit. I didn't think much of it, but when she rolled up the door to the unit, I was floored. Inside were blue bags filled with clothes. I had no idea she was running a full-blown reselling business. I'd heard her mention needing to "run to the storage unit" before, but I didn't realize the scale of it.

Curious, I asked her to break it down for me. She explained that she bought gently used clothes from places like Plato's Closet and other second-hand shops and resold them on platforms like eBay and Poshmark. The system was simple but effective. As she laid it all out, a vision began to form in my mind. This business had incredible potential, and with a few adjustments, I could see it scaling massively. I asked if she'd be open to a partnership, and she agreed, as long as it made sense for the both of us.

The next day, we hit the ground running. She took me to Plato's Closet and other consignment shops in D.C., where she taught me how to select items using an app to gauge their resale value. But the real breakthrough came when she introduced me to the Goodwill warehouse in

Catonsville, MD, where they sold clothes by the pound—$0.99 per pound, to be exact. It was harder work, but the profit margins were lucrative.

I spent hours digging through bins and left with a decent haul. Back at her place, we processed the items, and I quickly realized that while some of my picks were damaged, the cashmere sweaters I found would sell for a nice profit. That night, I knew this business had serious potential, but I also knew we needed better sources.

CHAPTER 7

From Goodwill to Greatness: Scaling the Operation

Expanding Beyond Local Resale to Build a Resale Empire
The first thing that came to mind was New York City —fashion capital, dense population, and limited storage space. That meant more donations of high-quality clothes. I planned a trip to visit my mother in Queens, but I had another mission: to explore Goodwill warehouses in the city.

The adrenaline rush I got from finding so many amazing deals at Goodwill was indescribable. I couldn't believe my luck in stumbling on this hidden gem of resellers. As I navigated through the store, I was amazed by the hustle and bustle of the underground community of resellers. It was like a secret society that only a select few knew about. I watched in awe as teams of people worked together, combing through bins with expert precision. It was like watching a well-oiled machine in action.

As I made my way through the store, I noticed that everyone had their own niche. Some were on the lookout for designer shoes, while others were searching for high-end handbags. And then there were the bulk buyers, who were scouring for unique pieces to ship overseas to high-end boutiques. It was a whole new world that I had never been exposed to before. And I couldn't believe that I had stumbled upon it by following my instincts.

After hours of shopping, my mother and I walked out with over 50 high-quality items, including three vintage pieces that I couldn't wait to add to my own wardrobe. And the best part? I had spent less than $100. I couldn't believe the amazing deals I had scored, and I knew that this was just the beginning of my journey into the world of reselling.

With this new inventory, I streamlined the process— optimizing our listing times and outsourcing some tasks to a team in the Philippines. Within two weeks, we scaled up from one small storage unit to three much larger units. The business was growing fast, and it felt like there was no limit to how far we could go.

CHAPTER 8

Going Global: The Paris Discovery

How a Trip to Paris Sparked a Passion for Luxury and Crypto
As the business scaled, I began exploring the luxury resale market. In early 2018, I took a trip to Paris, France, to source high-end, luxury-brand clothes. Paris, the fashion capital of the world, didn't disappoint. I discovered thrift stores and donation centers similar to Goodwill but filled with luxury brands that commanded premium prices back in the U.S.

The trip wasn't just about sourcing inventory. Paris opened my eyes to a world far beyond resale. I fell in love with the city's architecture, food, and culture. More importantly, I met people deeply entrenched in the **crypto space**[7], with a global perspective on cryptocurrency and blockchain. It became clear to me that most of the world, especially back in the U.S., was lagging behind in truly understanding the transformative potential of these technologies.

This experience ignited a passion within me. I returned from Paris more determined than ever. While the resale business was booming, I knew that crypto was the key to unlocking generational wealth. I just had to figure out how to leverage it.

CHAPTER 9

The Return to Bitcoin and the Introduction to Altcoins

Exploring New Frontiers Beyond Bitcoin
Even though I was finding success in the resale business, my instinct to hustle kept pushing me to seek out the next big opportunity. Bitcoin had already proven that the digital gold rush was real, and I didn't want to miss the next wave of wealth creation. That's when I began exploring **altcoins**[8] —those alternative cryptocurrencies beyond Bitcoin, such as **Dogecoin, Ethereum, Litecoin,** and **XRP**[9].

Venturing into altcoins opened my eyes to the fact that there was so much more to the world of cryptocurrency than just Bitcoin. While Bitcoin may have been the pioneer, there were countless other coins with unique features and potential for growth. I was fascinated by the diverse applications of blockchain technology and how it was revolutionizing industries beyond just finance. From supply chain management to healthcare and voting systems, the potential for blockchain seemed endless.

My journey into altcoins also led me to discover the power of the community behind each coin. I joined online forums and social media groups dedicated to discussing and analyzing different altcoins. I was amazed by the level of passion and knowledge shared by these individuals, and it opened my eyes to the collaborative nature of the cryptocurrency world. I realized that it wasn't just about making quick profits, but also about being a part of a larger community dedicated to driving innovation and change.

As I continued to explore new frontiers beyond Bitcoin, I also became more aware of the risks involved in the cryptocurrency market. I learned to approach every investment with caution and do thorough research before making any decisions. I also started diversifying my portfolio to mitigate potential losses. The journey was not without its challenges, but it was also incredibly rewarding. It opened my mind to the endless possibilities of cryptocurrency and left me excited for what the future holds.

CHAPTER 10

The Blockchain Revelation

Unveiling the True Power Behind Cryptocurrency

If cryptocurrencies were the trains carrying value, blockchain was the track they rode on. While Bitcoin hogged the headlines, the real hero of the revolution was blockchain. It wasn't just the foundation for Bitcoin—it powered every cryptocurrency and had the potential to disrupt industries far beyond finance.

The deeper I explored, the clearer it became that blockchain wasn't just about digital money. It was a technology poised to reshape entire industries, revolutionize **data ownership**[10], and transform how we communicate and transfer value in the digital age. Blockchain could revolutionize everything from healthcare and supply chains to real estate and even voting systems.

The realization hit me like a ton of bricks: blockchain was as monumental as the invention of the internet, the printing press, or even fire. Its potential to change the world wasn't limited to finance—it would impact how we live, work, and interact on a global scale.

Before diving into the 4th Industrial Revolution, **The Great Reset**[11], and the role blockchain will play in shaping the future, it's essential to take a step back. The story of Bitcoin and blockchain is part of a much larger narrative: the evolution of money itself.

CHAPTER 11

The Evolution of Money: From Bartering to Bitcoin

Understanding How the Concept of Money Has Evolved Over Time

Money has evolved in ways that are beyond our imagination. As Bitcoin enters the scene, it revolutionizes the way we view money and its role in our daily lives. This digital currency is not just a means of exchange but a symbol of change and progress. The concept of money has come a long way, from ancient bartering systems to the decentralized economy of Bitcoin.

For thousands of years, money has been an essential part of human society. It has shaped civilizations, economies, and even cultures. The bartering system, where goods and services were exchanged directly, was the first form of money. As societies grew and became more complex, precious metals such as gold and silver were used as a medium of exchange. Later, paper money and coins were introduced, which made transactions easier and more efficient. However, with the rise of technology, the concept of money has evolved even further.

Today, we have digital currencies like Bitcoin, which operate independently of any central authority. This has opened up a whole new world of possibilities, where people can transact with each other directly without the need for intermediaries. Bitcoin's revolutionary nature has shown us that the concept of money is constantly evolving, and it will continue to do so in the future.

The Age of Barter: Trading Goods and Services

Before money existed, people relied on bartering to trade goods and services. The system worked on one basic principle: if I had something you wanted and you had something I needed, we could make a trade. Simple, right? But there was a big problem called the "double coincidence of wants." For a trade to happen, both parties had to want what the other had—and at the same time.

Imagine trying to trade a hunting spear for a sack of grain, but the person with the grain had no use for your spear. This inefficiency made bartering impractical as societies grew more complex, so people needed a more universal system of value exchange.

Physical Objects as Money: The First Currency

By 3000 BCE, cultures around the world had adopted physical objects as money. Cowrie shells in Africa, silver rings in Mesopotamia, and wampum beads among Native American tribes became the first widely accepted currencies. These objects offered a common standard of value, simplifying trade. But carrying bags of shells or metal pieces became impractical as economies expanded, which led to the creation of coins.

Coins and Paper Money: The Birth of Modern Currency

Around 600 BCE, Lydia (modern-day Turkey) minted the first coins made from precious metals like gold and silver. These coins were durable, portable, and universally accepted, boosting trade across continents. By the 7th century CE, China introduced the first form of paper money, revolutionizing long-distance trade by making it easier to transport value over vast distances.

As paper currency spread globally, it transformed economies. But even paper money faced challenges as financial systems evolved.

The Gold Standard: A New Era of Trust

By the 19th century, the global economy relied on the gold standard—a system where a country's currency was directly tied to its gold reserves. This system provided trust and stability in international commerce. However, economic crises in the 20th century led countries to abandon the gold standard, with the U.S. officially moving away from it in 1971, ushering in the fiat currency era, where money was no longer backed by physical commodities like gold.

The mid-20th century brought about credit cards, making money even more abstract. Consumers could buy now and pay later, fueling spending and economic growth. The 21st century saw the rise of digital transactions through services like PayPal, Apple Pay, and digital **wallets**[12], making financial transactions faster and more global.

Yet, despite these advancements, the financial system remained centralized—controlled by banks, governments, and corporations. This centralized control carried risks, including corruption, inflation, and loss of privacy. A new solution was needed.

The Dawn of Decentralized Money: Enter Bitcoin

In 2009, everything changed. Bitcoin, introduced by the mysterious figure **Satoshi Nakamoto**[13], became the world's first decentralized digital currency. Unlike traditional currency, no government, bank, or institution controlled it. Powered by blockchain technology, Bitcoin allowed people to send money directly to each other without intermediaries like banks.

Bitcoin solved several key issues that had plagued traditional financial systems—double-spending (spending the same money twice), high transaction fees, and limited accessibility. More importantly, it changed how we think about money. Value could transfer and store independently of government or bank control for the first time, resulting in a more democratic and decentralized financial system.

What started as a niche project soon became a global movement, paving the way for an entire ecosystem of cryptocurrencies and decentralized finance **(DeFi)**[14].

CHAPTER 12

The Next Frontier: Embracing the Future of Money

How Bitcoin and Blockchain Are Shaping the Future of Finance

From bartering to Bitcoin, the history of money is filled with innovation and adaptation in response to the ever-evolving needs of society. Each transition, from physical currency to digital transactions, has fundamentally altered the way we conduct business, build trust, and perceive wealth. Now, with the emergence of Bitcoin and blockchain technology, we are witnessing the next major leap in this evolution.

Beyond being a new form of currency, Bitcoin and blockchain have the potential to transform the very foundations of finance, ownership, and trust. But their impact extends far beyond just these industries. With its decentralized, secure, and transparent nature, blockchain technology has the power to revolutionize a wide range of sectors, from supply chain management to healthcare. This is only possible because of the underlying mechanics of blockchain, which we will explore in more detail in the next chapter.

As we enter the era of the 4th Industrial Revolution, it is clear that blockchain is at the forefront of this transformation. Its potential to disrupt and innovate is vast, and its applications are only just beginning to be explored. From the story of money to the future of commerce, the impact of blockchain and Bitcoin is far-reaching and ever-growing. So stay tuned, because the story is far from over.

CHAPTER 13

The Backbone of Bitcoin: Understanding Blockchain Technology

The Engine Driving the Digital Revolution

When I first got into Bitcoin, it seemed like another quick way to make some cash. After all, who doesn't love the idea of turning a few hundred bucks into six figures? But after that lucky break in 2017, I realized something much bigger was happening. That win wasn't just a fluke—it was the byproduct of a technology I barely understood at the time. As I dug deeper, it became clear: Bitcoin is just the tip of the iceberg. The real revolution is the engine behind it all—blockchain.

The more I learned, the more I realized that blockchain wasn't just about cryptocurrency. It was about creating a system that could fundamentally change how we interact with money, data, and trust. In the world of crypto, Bitcoin is the flash, but blockchain is the foundation. Without it, none of this would be possible. As I began to understand it better, I realized this technology has the power to reshape not just finance but entire industries. The question is... Are you ready for it?

In this chapter, we'll break down blockchain from the ground up. We will sift through the buzzwords and hype to explore the true revolutionary nature of this technology.

By the end, you'll understand that blockchain isn't just a tool for tech insiders—it's the backbone of the future.

A New Kind of Ledger

How Blockchain Replaces Traditional Record-Keeping
To grasp blockchain's full impact, we need to revisit a familiar concept: **ledgers**[15]. Blockchain technology has revolutionized the way we record transactions and store data. The traditional centralized ledgers, which have been used for centuries, have now been replaced by decentralized ledgers, also known as blockchains. These ledgers are distributed across a network of computers, creating a secure and transparent system.

The centralization of traditional ledgers posed a significant risk, as a single entity controlled all the data. This meant that if the entity was compromised, the entire system could fail, resulting in lost data and trust. With blockchain, the ledger is distributed across multiple nodes, eliminating the risk of a single point of failure. This makes it almost impossible for any data to be tampered with or lost. The decentralized nature of blockchain also eliminates the need for third-party intermediaries, such as banks or governments.

This reduces the risk of errors, corruption, and manipulation, which can occur with centralized systems. Blockchain ensures that every transaction is verified by the entire network, making it a highly secure and trustworthy system. By removing the need for intermediaries, blockchain also speeds up the transaction process, making it more efficient and cost-effective.

How Blockchain Works: The Block and the Chain

Understanding the Core Structure of Blockchain Technology
The term "blockchain" perfectly describes the structure: a chain of blocks. Each block contains a group of transactions, which are verified and sealed by the network. Once confirmed, the block is added to the chain, permanently locking it in place. This creates an unbreakable, transparent, and chronological record of transactions. This revolutionary technology has been the driving force behind the digital revolution, transforming the way we conduct transactions online.

But blockchain is not just limited to Bitcoin transactions. It has the potential to revolutionize various industries, such as supply chain management, healthcare, and even voting systems. With its decentralized and transparent nature, blockchain has the power to eliminate intermediaries, reduce costs, and increase efficiency. This is why major tech companies, banks, and governments are exploring and investing in blockchain technology.

One of the most fascinating aspects of blockchain is its security. Blockchain is virtually unalterable, unlike traditional databases that are susceptible to hacking or manipulation. Blockchain links each block to its predecessor, forming an unalterable chain of blocks. This makes blockchain ideal for storing sensitive information, such as personal and financial data. As the digital revolution continues to gain momentum, blockchain is poised to play a crucial role in shaping the future of technology and our society.

Why Was Blockchain Necessary for Bitcoin?

How Blockchain Solves Bitcoin's Biggest Challenges

One of Bitcoin's biggest challenges was the issue of trust. In traditional financial systems, we rely on banks or payment processors to verify transactions and prevent things like **double-spending**[16]. Bitcoin was designed to remove the need for these intermediaries, enabling peer-to-peer transactions. Blockchain is what makes this possible.

Blockchain's decentralized nature ensures that no single entity controls Bitcoin transactions. Instead, every transaction is recorded, verified, and stored on the blockchain, making the system transparent and trustworthy. This allows anyone, anywhere in the world, to send and receive money without needing a central authority. This is a significant advancement compared to traditional financial systems, where trust is placed on intermediaries such as banks and payment processors. These intermediaries not only add additional costs to transactions but also create a centralized point of control, making the system vulnerable to manipulation and fraud. Moreover, the use of blockchain technology in Bitcoin has solved the issue of double-spending, which has been a major challenge for digital currencies.

Double-spending is the act of trying to spend the same digital currency more than once, which is prevented by blockchain's ability to record and verify every transaction. This is because, on the blockchain, every transaction is linked to the previous one, forming a chain of blocks, making it virtually impossible to alter or duplicate a transaction. This has made Bitcoin a secure and reliable means of peer-to-peer transactions without the need for intermediaries. In addition to trust and double-spending, another challenge that blockchain has solved for Bitcoin is the issue of transaction fees.

In traditional financial systems, intermediaries charge fees for their services, which can vary depending on the transaction's size and speed. However, with blockchain technology, transactions can be done without the need for intermediaries, reducing transaction costs significantly. This has made Bitcoin a more accessible and cost-effective option for individuals and businesses worldwide, further driving its adoption and growth.

Blockchain: Beyond Bitcoin

Revolutionizing Industries with Decentralized Solutions

Blockchain technology has been gaining widespread attention and adoption due to its potential to revolutionize industries. While Bitcoin was the first application of blockchain, its uses extend far beyond cryptocurrency. With its decentralized and secure nature, blockchain has the potential to transform industries such as finance, supply chain management, healthcare, and more. One of the key benefits of blockchain technology is its ability to create secure and transparent systems. As a result, more and more businesses are exploring the use of blockchain to streamline their operations and improve customer experiences.

Blockchain technology also has the potential to disrupt traditional business models by creating new and innovative solutions. For example, using smart contracts on the blockchain can automate and streamline processes, reducing the need for manual labor and increasing efficiency. This has the potential to create new job opportunities and improve the overall functioning of industries. With its potential to transform and improve various industries, blockchain is here to stay and will continue to drive innovation and growth in the future.

Supply Chain Transparency: The increasing need for manual labor and efficiency in industries has led to the adoption of innovative technologies like blockchain. This revolutionary technology has the potential to not only streamline processes but also provide a transparent and tamper-proof record of every step in a product's journey. Blockchain can greatly improve supply chain management in industries such as food and retail. This not only increases efficiency but also instills trust and confidence in consumers, leading to improved overall functioning of the industries.

In addition to supply chain management, blockchain has the potential to transform and improve various other industries as well. Its decentralized nature and secure, immutable records make it ideal for industries that require high levels of data security, such as healthcare and finance. This technology has the power to drive innovation and growth in these industries by providing solutions to long-standing challenges and improving processes. With its many use cases and benefits, it is clear that blockchain is here to stay.

Healthcare Records: Additionally, blockchain technology can assist in managing complex insurance claims and ensuring accurate billing in the healthcare industry. By recording all transactions on an immutable ledger, the potential for fraud and errors is drastically reduced, saving both time and money for all parties involved. This level of data security can also benefit patients by protecting their sensitive personal and financial information.

Overall, the adoption of blockchain technology in

industries such as healthcare has the potential to bring about significant improvements and advancements. With its ability to provide secure and transparent data storage, streamline processes, and reduce costs, blockchain is set to drive innovation and growth in these industries for years to come. Its disruptive potential is undeniable.

Decentralized Voting: Blockchain could revolutionize voting by providing a secure, transparent, and tamper-proof way to cast ballots, eliminating voter fraud, and ensuring the integrity of elections—which is crucial for any democracy.

Perhaps one of the most exciting applications is **smart contracts**[18], self-executing contracts where the terms are written directly into code. For example, a smart contract could automatically release payment once a product is delivered, without the need for intermediaries like lawyers or banks. This innovation has the potential to disrupt industries like insurance, real estate, and finance by streamlining processes and reducing costs.

Did You Know?

Mainstream Companies Are Embracing Blockchain
As blockchain continues to evolve, major tech companies like Google are forming partnerships with blockchain projects. When tech giants get involved, it's clear that this isn't just a passing trend—it's the future. One of Google's most notable partnerships is with **Solana**[18], a blockchain known for its speed and scalability. Solana's fast-growing market cap, scalable network, and partnerships make it a key player in blockchain's future.

Google Cloud now provides real-time data from Solana,

integrating decentralized networks with cloud computing. This partnership enhances Solana's scalability and provides developers with opportunities to create more advanced applications. This move not only signifies a partnership, but also signifies the integration of blockchain technology into the core infrastructure of major tech companies.

Google has also partnered with Hedera **(HBAR)**[18], a blockchain platform focused on fast, secure, and decentralized enterprise applications. These partnerships illustrate how blockchain is being woven into the fabric of mainstream tech, and the opportunities for innovation are vast.

Google's Blockchain Play and the Path Forward

How Big Tech is Shaping the Blockchain Future
A company like Google's investment in blockchain signals a clear direction for the future. These partnerships with Solana and Hedera represent the beginning of blockchain's integration into mainstream tech infrastructure. As blockchain and cloud systems blend, the potential for innovation will only grow.

For those who are paying attention, this creates a unique opportunity to get involved early. Blockchain is driving the 4th Industrial Revolution, from decentralized finance to next-gen digital infrastructure, and the opportunities are still open for those ready to dive in. But make no mistake—the window to get in early is closing fast.

A Paradigm Shift

Blockchain's Role in Redefining Trust, Ownership, and Value

Blockchain has the potential to significantly transform the digital landscape and the way we interact with one another. It represents a paradigm shift in our understanding of trust, ownership, and value exchange. Just as the internet transformed how we communicate and access information, blockchain is set to redefine trust, ownership, and value exchange in the digital age. Blockchain isn't just about money—it's about building decentralized systems where trust is coded into the infrastructure. The power of blockchain lies in its ability to create decentralized systems that are secure, transparent, and immutable. By using advanced cryptography and distributed ledger technology, blockchain eliminates the need for intermediaries and provides a more efficient and trustworthy way to transfer assets and information.

While there are still challenges to be overcome, such as scalability and regulatory hurdles, the momentum of blockchain is unstoppable. Those who understand and embrace this technology now will have the opportunity to shape its future and be at the forefront of this digital revolution. We are just at the beginning of this journey, and the potential for blockchain to redefine trust, ownership, and value exchange is vast. As we continue to see its implementation and adoption, the impact of blockchain will only continue to grow.

Now that we've explored blockchain, you can see how this technology goes far beyond Bitcoin. It's the key to understanding the future of finance, trust, and transparency. Blockchain has opened doors to countless possibilities, and its impact is just beginning to unfold. It's remarkable how such a seemingly simple concept can have such far-reaching and transformative effects. With blockchain, we can now secure our data and assets in a way that was once thought to be impossible. This has the potential to revolutionize the way we do business and interact with one another.

In the next chapter, we'll dive deeper into how these partnerships and technological advances are shaping the evolution of the digital economy. This is where we see the true power of blockchain in action. By tracking where the major players are focusing their efforts, we can begin to see the future of finance, governance, and ownership. It's exciting to think about how this technology can empower individuals and organizations alike to control their assets and data. With blockchain, we are entering a new era of decentralization and transparency, and the possibilities are endless.

As we continue to explore the potential of blockchain, it's important to keep in mind that this technology is still in its early stages. We are only scratching the surface of what it can do, and there will undoubtedly be challenges and obstacles along the way. However, the potential for positive change and disruption is immense, and it's up to us to harness it for the greater good. The engine driving the digital revolution may have just started, but its impact is already being felt, and we have only just begun to see its true potential.

CHAPTER 14

Wallets, Keys, and Storage: Securing Your Digital Assets in the New Frontier

Mastering the Tools for a Decentralized World

When I first stepped into the world of cryptocurrency, one of the most confusing aspects was how to store my digital assets securely. With traditional money, it's simple: you either put it in a bank or a safe at home. But in the realm of digital currencies, the concept of wallets, keys, and storage is a bit more complex. In this chapter, we'll break it all down—what wallets are, how they work, and why understanding them is vital as we move into **Web3**[20], the **Internet of Things (IoT)**[21], and the 4th Industrial Revolution (4IR). I'll share personal tips and analogies that helped me make sense of it all.

My First Wallet: A Bank Account and a Safe at Home

Making Sense of Hot and Cold Wallets

When I first started in crypto, learning about wallets felt like trying to decipher a new language. But I found a way to simplify it for myself and others. Think of a **hot wallet**[22] like your bank account—connected to the internet, always ready for transactions, but exposed to risks like hacking. Whereas, on the other hand, a **cold wallet**[23] is like the shoebox or safe you keep at home. It's offline, making it much harder to access remotely but less convenient for everyday use.

In this chapter, I'll explain how balancing accessibility and security is crucial when managing your digital assets, whether you're a casual trader or deeply invested in the crypto space.

Hot Wallets: Your Everyday Bank Account

Convenience with a Side of Risk

A hot wallet is similar to a bank account—it's connected to the internet and designed for daily use. Whether you're trading on an exchange or interacting with Web3 applications like DeFi or NFTs[24], a hot wallet gives you immediate access to your funds. However, this ease of access comes with risks. Just like your bank account can be hacked, so can a hot wallet. That's why most people only keep small amounts of cryptocurrency in their hot wallets —just enough for daily transactions.

If you're heavily involved in decentralized finance or NFT trading, you'll need a hot wallet, but always keep security in mind. It's convenient but vulnerable in the broader Web3 ecosystem.

Pros:
- Easy for daily transactions.
- Immediate access to DeFi platforms, NFTs, and exchanges.
- Integrates with many Web3 applications.

Cons:
- Vulnerable to hacking and phishing attacks.

- Not ideal for storing large amounts of cryptocurrency.

Cold Wallets: Your Shoebox for Long-Term Storage

The Ultimate Security Solution

Just like you wouldn't keep all your savings in a checking account, you shouldn't keep all your crypto in a hot wallet. For long-term storage, consider using a cold wallet, similar to a **shoebox**[25] or safe where you store your cash at home. Cold wallets are typically hardware devices that remain offline, making them far more secure against digital theft. If you're holding Bitcoin, Ethereum, or other assets for the long term, a cold wallet is essential.

Cold wallets aren't as convenient, though. Accessing your funds requires plugging the device into a computer or transferring them back to a hot wallet. But for those who prioritize security, this trade-off is worth it.

Pros:
- Offline storage makes it safe from hackers.
- Ideal for long-term holders (HODLers).

Cons:
- Not suited for daily transactions.
- Requires effort to access compared to hot wallets.

Public and Private Keys: Your Email and Password

Mastering the Key to Digital Security

This was confusing for me at first, but I came up with an easy analogy. Your **public key**[26] is like your email address —it's what you give out so people can send you assets. It's public and can be shared freely. Your **private key**[27], though, is like your password—you never share this with anyone. If someone has your private key, they have full control of your assets, just like someone with your password can access your email.

Public keys let others send you cryptocurrency, while private keys ensure that only you can control those funds. As we dive deeper into Web3, where personal data control is crucial, mastering the use of public and private keys will be essential to safely participating in the digital revolution.

Understanding Keys:

Pros:

- Public keys make transactions seamless.
- Private keys offer unmatched security.

Cons:

- Lose your private keys, your funds are lost permanently.
- Managing keys can be tricky for beginners.

The Future of Wallets: IoT and 4IR Integration

Wallets as Gateways to the Internet of Things

As we advance into the Fourth Industrial Revolution, wallets are evolving beyond just storing crypto—they're becoming gateways into the Internet of Things (IoT). Imagine a future where your smart car, home, and appliances are all connected via blockchain. You'll be able to pay for tolls, groceries, or repairs automatically through smart contracts, and your crypto wallet will handle these micro-transactions effortlessly.

As our world continues to advance, blockchain technology is evolving and becoming increasingly prevalent. Blockchain technology is not only storing cryptocurrencies, but it is also expanding into the Internet of Things. No longer will you have to worry about multiple transactions and payments, as smart contracts will handle everything for you. But blockchain is not just a means of storing money. It has the potential to hold so much more—data, contracts, and even identities.

This is the future of digital ownership, and it is rapidly becoming a reality. The convergence of blockchain, IoT, and Web3 will give us unparalleled control over our interactions with technology. With this level of connectivity and automation, our lives will become more streamlined and efficient. The possibilities are endless, and the potential for growth is immense.

Wallet Evolution and Regulatory Oversight

The Growing Role of Governments and Corporations in Crypto

Just like how gaming has evolved from Atari to PlayStation 5, wallets in the digital space are evolving. Companies like Sony and Microsoft are already filing patents for blockchain technology, enabling users to own digital assets like NFTs or in-game items. These corporations recognize that crypto and blockchain are driving the future of gaming and ownership.

Governments are also stepping in, introducing regulations like **KYC (Know Your Customer)**[28] and **AML (Anti Money Laundering)**[29] for digital wallets. While these regulations raise privacy concerns, they also pave the way for more secure and widespread adoption of cryptocurrency.

PayPal and Ledger Are Transforming Wallet Security

Traditional Finance Meets Decentralized Technology

The partnership between **PayPal**[30] and **Ledger**[31] is a significant step in making cryptocurrency more accessible and secure. PayPal, one of the largest digital payment platforms, now allows users to buy, sell, and hold digital assets like Bitcoin and Ethereum. By integrating with Ledger, a leader in hardware wallets, PayPal users can now enjoy the convenience of a hot wallet with the added security of cold storage

This collaboration bridges the gap for millions of users who are hesitant to enter the crypto world. PayPal's hot wallet acts like a bank account, while Ledger's cold wallet functions like a secure safe at home, offering both accessibility and protection for long-term investments.

Balancing Security and Access in the New Digital Economy

How to Secure Your Digital Assets

Managing wallets, keys, and storage is all about balancing security and accessibility. In this digital frontier, understanding how wallets work—both hot and cold—is crucial for anyone engaging with cryptocurrency, Web3, or the 4IR. As technology evolves, so do the tools we use to secure our assets. From cold storage to smart contracts, knowing how to manage your assets safely will empower you in this decentralized future.

The full potential of blockchain extends beyond Bitcoin. In the next chapter, **From Bitcoin to Ethereum: A New Era of Blockchain Innovation**[32], we'll explore how Ethereum is pushing the boundaries even further. Ethereum isn't just a cryptocurrency—it's a platform that enables developers to create decentralized applications, smart contracts, and entire digital ecosystems. If Bitcoin was revolutionary, get ready to see how Ethereum is transforming what blockchain can truly accomplish.

CHAPTER 15

The Rise of Altcoins: Expanding the Blockchain Universe

Exploring the Diversity of Digital Assets

When I first entered the crypto space, it quickly became clear that not all digital assets were created equal. Some, like Bitcoin, represented a revolution in decentralized finance, while others, like Ethereum, showcased the versatility of blockchain. As the market evolved, I began to notice two distinct categories of cryptocurrencies: **stablecoins**[33] and **meme tokens**[34]. Stablecoins offered a sense of reliability amidst crypto's volatility, while meme tokens thrived on community-driven hype, often leading to extreme price swings. This contrast between stability and speculation was fascinating and highlighted just how unpredictable and diverse the crypto world could be.

Witnessing the power of both stablecoins and meme tokens, I realized that understanding this spectrum was essential for navigating the broader crypto ecosystem. In this chapter, we'll dive into how these two types of digital assets are shaping the future of cryptocurrency and why their contrasting purposes make the space so dynamic.

Utility in Action: Stablecoins vs. Meme Tokens

Stability or Speculation? The Cryptocurrency Contradiction

The crypto landscape is filled with contradictions. On one

side, you have projects focused on utility, stability, and long-term sustainability, like stablecoins, which provide a safe harbor from volatility. On the other hand, you have meme tokens—coins that often started as jokes but have evolved into their own cultural phenomena, fueled by hype, internet culture, and community-driven momentum.

For every stablecoin offering security and predictability, there's a **Dogecoin**[35] or **Shiba Inu**[36] that rides the waves of meme culture, creating millionaires overnight and crashing just as fast. Let's explore how. We'll explore how both stablecoins and meme tokens are influencing the future of crypto and why the balance between their purposes makes this space so unique.

The Need for Stability: The Rise of Stablecoins

Why Stablecoins Are Vital to the Crypto Ecosystem

As the cryptocurrency market matured, it became clear that a stable asset was needed to counter the volatility of cryptos like Bitcoin and Ethereum. The dramatic price swings of these assets made them unreliable as mediums of exchange or stores of value. That's where stablecoins come in. Stablecoins are cryptocurrencies designed to maintain a stable value, often pegged to reserve assets like fiat currencies, such as the U.S. dollar.

Key Purposes of Stablecoins:

- **Hedging Against Volatility:** Stablecoins offer a safe harbor for traders and investors, allowing them to exit volatile positions without converting back to fiat currencies.

- **Facilitating Transactions:** Stablecoins enable

rapid transactions within and across exchanges, especially in the decentralized finance (DeFi) ecosystem.

• **Cross-Border Payments:** They provide a low-cost, fast alternative for international payments and remittances.

• **Smart Contract Utility:** Stablecoins are widely used in smart contracts, lending protocols, and DeFi platforms as collateral or liquidity providers.

Types of Stablecoins

Understanding the Mechanisms Behind Stability
There are three main types of stablecoins, each with a unique approach to maintaining price stability:

• **Fiat-Collateralized Stablecoins:** Backed by fiat currencies like USD or EUR held in reserves (e.g., USDT37, USDC38).

• **Crypto-Collateralized Stablecoins:** Backed by other cryptocurrencies (e.g., DAI39), often over-collateralized to manage volatility.

• **Algorithmic Stablecoins:** Use algorithms and smart contracts to control token supply and maintain a stable price. These are more experimental and have faced challenges in keeping their pegs.

The Top 5 Most Popular Stablecoins

Reliable, Liquid, and Essential to Crypto

1. Tether (USDT)

Market Cap: ~$83 billion (early 2024)[40].
Pros: High liquidity, widely accepted.

Cons: Concerns about transparency and reserve backing.

2. USD Coin (USDC)

Market Cap: ~$40 billion (early 2024)[41].
Pros: Transparent, regular audits.
Cons: Centralized control.

3. Binance USD (BUSD)

Market Cap: ~$25 billion (early 2024)[42].
Pros: Regulatory approval, strong liquidity.
Cons: Reliant on Binance's reputation.

4. Dai (DAI)

Market Cap: ~$8 billion (early 2024)[43].

Pros: Decentralized, governed by **MakerDAO**[44].
Cons: Complexity and collateral volatility.

5. TrueUSD (TUSD)

Market Cap: ~$4 billion (early 2024)[45].
Pros: Transparent, straightforward.
Cons: Lower liquidity compared to USDT and USDC.

The Rise of Meme Tokens: Popularity and Volatility

Where Hype Meets Extreme Price Swings
On the other end of the spectrum are meme tokens, driven by internet culture, social media hype, and community sentiment rather than any intrinsic value or utility. These tokens often start as jokes but can achieve massive gains, turning everyday investors into millionaires overnight. However, their speculative nature means they can also lead to significant losses just as quickly.

The Top 5 Most Popular Meme Tokens

Wildly Popular but Wildly Volatile

1. Dogecoin (DOGE)

Market Cap: ~$10 billion (early 2024)[46].
Pros: Strong community, widespread acceptance.
Cons: Minimal real-world use case, high volatility.

2. Shiba Inu (SHIB)

Market Cap: ~$6 billion (early 2024)[47].
Pros: Large following, DeFi integrations.
Cons: Extreme volatility, limited utility.

3. Pepe (PEPE)

Market Cap: ~$2 billion (early 2024)[48].
Pros: Quick to gain social traction.
Cons: Speculative with no real utility.

4. Floki Inu (FLOKI)

Market Cap: ~$1 billion (early 2024)[49].
Pros: Strong branding, and community-driven marketing.
Cons: Minimal real-world application, highly speculative.

5. Baby DogeCoin (BabyDoge)

Market Cap: ~$800 million (early 2024)[50].
Pros: Large and active community.
Cons: Limited utility and extreme volatility.

The Paradox of Usefulness vs. Speculation

The Irony of Crypto: Stablecoins vs. Meme Tokens

The contrast between utility-driven stablecoins and speculative meme tokens reveals a fundamental irony in the crypto space.

- **Stablecoins:** Stablecoins, such as Tether and USD Coin, are the backbone of the crypto world. They provide the much-needed stability and liquidity for various use cases in the ecosystem. Stablecoins are crucial for DeFi, allowing users to easily swap between different assets and access lending and borrowing services. They are also widely used for trading, providing a safe haven during times of market volatility. Additionally, stablecoins play a significant role in cross-border transactions, offering a faster and cheaper alternative to traditional methods.

- **Meme Tokens:** On the flip side, meme tokens, despite offering minimal utility, often attract the most speculative trading and wild price fluctuations, creating opportunities for rapid wealth creation—and destruction.

In this chapter, we explored the contrasting landscape of stablecoins and meme tokens, highlighting the unique balance between utility and speculation in the crypto world. Stablecoins provide a foundation for decentralized finance (DeFi), offering stability and liquidity, while meme tokens ride the waves of community-driven hype, often leading to volatile gains and losses. These two elements represent the broader diversity and complexity of the cryptocurrency market, where navigating between stability and speculation is a critical skill for any investor.

Now, we turn our attention to the larger forces shaping

this landscape. If you want to know where the future of finance is headed, it's essential to follow the moves of the world's most influential players. The World Economic Forum (WEF) and other global organizations like the International Monetary Fund (IMF), the World Health Organization (WHO), and the World Trade Organization (WTO) are leading the charge in shaping the future of the global economy.

Their focus on blockchain, cryptocurrencies, and decentralized technologies shows that this is more than just a trend—it's a revolution. The 4th Industrial Revolution (4IR), driven by innovations in blockchain, AI, and IoT, is reshaping every aspect of how we work, live, and interact.

In the next chapter, we'll dive deeper into the role of the WEF and how they, along with other global organizations, are influencing the 4IR. We'll explore how these power players are navigating the complexities of blockchain, digital currencies, and the push for central bank digital currencies (CBDCs) and what this means for the future of wealth and governance.

CHAPTER 16

Following the Leaders: The Power Elite's
Vision for Blockchain and the 4IR

The World Economic Forum: A Blueprint for the Future

When I first entered the world of cryptocurrency, I quickly learned that understanding technology alone wasn't enough to predict where the market was headed. You had to follow the movements of the global power elite—the key players who shape economic policy and innovation. These decision-makers sit in boardrooms, often out of the public eye, but their actions send ripples across the world. Among the most influential of these power players is the World Economic Forum (WEF). By keeping an eye on the WEF and other global organizations, we can trace the breadcrumbs that lead to the future of blockchain, cryptocurrency, and the Fourth Industrial Revolution (4IR).

The World Economic Forum (WEF), established in 1971 by Professor Klaus Schwab, is an international platform where leaders from various sectors—government, business, academia, and civil society—gather to discuss the global issues shaping tomorrow's world. Based in Geneva, Switzerland, the WEF's mission is to "improve the state of the world" through public-private cooperation. The annual Davos meeting, held in a small mountain town in Switzerland, has become synonymous with elite decision-making and forward-thinking discussions on everything from climate change to technological innovation.

The WEF sees the 4th Industrial Revolution not just as a wave of new technologies but as a fundamental shift in how we live, work, and govern. From artificial intelligence (AI) to blockchain, these innovations are dismantling traditional systems and creating new ones in their place. At the heart of this transformation is blockchain, a technology that the WEF believes will be foundational to the new digital economy.

The WEF's Vision: Blockchain as the Backbone of the 4IR

The WEF doesn't see blockchain merely as a tool for cryptocurrency—it sees it as a pivotal technology for reshaping industries across the board. Blockchain's decentralized and transparent nature allows for the secure transfer of value and data without intermediaries, making it a key component of the WEF's vision for the 4IR. The organization has consistently emphasized the wide-reaching implications of blockchain, predicting its transformative impact across various sectors, from supply chains to financial services, healthcare, and governance.

One of the most significant contributions of blockchain, according to the WEF, is its ability to decentralize trust. Traditionally, trust has been centralized in institutions like banks, governments, and corporations. However, blockchain enables trust to be distributed across a network, reducing the need for intermediaries and increasing transparency. This decentralization of trust has the potential to disrupt existing power structures and create more equitable systems.

Key Areas of Blockchain Impact According to the WEF

While blockchain's most well-known application is in cryptocurrency, the WEF recognizes its potential to revolutionize numerous other areas. Here are the key areas where the WEF predicts blockchain will have the most significant impact.

1. Supply Chain Transparency and Accountability

Global supply chains are often opaque and riddled with inefficiencies. Blockchain's ability to create a tamper-proof, transparent record of every transaction within a supply chain can significantly improve accountability. Companies can track goods from the source to the end consumer, ensuring ethical sourcing, reducing fraud, and increasing efficiency. This is especially important in industries such as food, fashion, and pharmaceuticals, where verifying the origin and journey of products is critical for both safety and ethical reasons.

2. Decentralized Finance (DeFi) and Financial Inclusion

One of blockchain's most exciting prospects is its potential to revolutionize the financial industry. Decentralized finance (DeFi) eliminates the need for traditional financial intermediaries like banks, enabling individuals to access financial services directly through decentralized networks. This is particularly significant for the billions of people worldwide who remain unbanked or underbanked. Blockchain provides a way for these individuals to participate in the global financial system, offering access to savings, loans, insurance, and investments without relying on traditional banking infrastructure.

3. Digital Identity and Data Privacy

In today's digital age, identity verification is more critical than ever. However, current systems often rely on centralized databases that are vulnerable to hacking and data breaches. Blockchain offers a solution by allowing individuals to control their digital identities through decentralized systems. This could revolutionize everything from voting systems to healthcare, ensuring that personal information is secure and only accessible to authorized parties.

4. Government and Governance Innovations

Governments around the world are exploring how blockchain can improve governance systems. From implementing smart contracts to creating Decentralized Autonomous Organizations (DAOs), blockchain offers new ways to manage resources and decision-making processes transparently. For instance, blockchain-based voting systems could eliminate fraud and ensure more democratic and transparent elections. Additionally, the use of smart contracts could streamline bureaucratic processes, reducing inefficiencies and corruption.

5. Environmental and Social Impact

Blockchain's potential to address global challenges extends beyond financial systems. The WEF has highlighted blockchain's role in combating climate change by improving the transparency and efficiency of carbon credit trading. Blockchain can also enhance social impact projects by ensuring that funds are used as intended, increasing accountability in charitable donations and development projects.

The Davos Agenda: Behind the Scenes at the WEF's Annual Meeting

The annual Davos meeting is where the WEF's vision for the future is discussed, debated, and refined. Attendees include heads of state, CEOs of the world's largest companies, and leading academics. The discussions that take place in Davos are not just theoretical—they are the blueprint for global policy and economic strategy. When blockchain first appeared on the Davos agenda, it was a signal that the technology had moved beyond the fringes and was being seriously considered as a foundational component of the future global economy.

While the formal agenda is packed with panels and discussions on the future of technology, finance, and governance, much of the real work happens behind closed doors. It's in these private meetings that deals are made, alliances are formed, and the future of industries is shaped. Understanding what's discussed at Davos gives us a glimpse into the strategies that the global elite are using to position themselves at the forefront of the 4IR.

Other Global Organizations Shaping Blockchain's Future

While the WEF leads the conversation on the 4IR, other global organizations are also recognizing the importance of blockchain and positioning themselves to leverage its transformative potential.

The International Monetary Fund (IMF): Central Bank Digital Currencies (CBDCs)

The IMF, whose mission is to stabilize the global

economy and promote financial cooperation, has become increasingly interested in blockchain's application to Central Bank Digital Currencies (CBDCs). CBDCs represent a digital form of a nation's fiat currency, issued and controlled by the central bank. Unlike decentralized cryptocurrencies like Bitcoin, CBDCs offer governments more control over their monetary policies while harnessing the benefits of digital currency, such as increased efficiency and reduced costs in financial transactions.

Countries such as China have already piloted their own CBDCs, with the digital Yuan leading the charge. The IMF is closely monitoring these developments, studying the implications of CBDCs for global trade, monetary policy, and financial inclusion. For many governments, CBDCs represent a way to maintain control in an increasingly decentralized financial world. However, they also offer a path toward bringing more people into the formal economy, particularly in regions where banking infrastructure is underdeveloped.

The World Trade Organization (WTO): Streamlining Global Trade

The WTO, responsible for overseeing global trade rules, views blockchain as a potential game-changer for international commerce. The organization is particularly interested in blockchain's ability to streamline trade processes, reduce paperwork, and increase transparency in cross-border transactions. By providing a secure and tamper-proof record of goods as they move through the supply chain, blockchain can help reduce fraud, ensure compliance with trade regulations, and improve the speed and efficiency of global trade.

Blockchain's application in trade extends beyond logistics. It could also play a critical role in intellectual property protection, ensuring that creators and innovators are fairly compensated for their work as it moves through global markets. The WTO is actively exploring these potentials through research and pilot projects, and it's clear that blockchain's role in global trade will continue to grow in the coming years.

The United Nations (UN): Blockchain for Social Good
The UN has recognized blockchain's potential to address pressing social issues, particularly in the areas of humanitarian aid and financial inclusion. The UN's World Food Programme has piloted blockchain systems to provide aid to refugees, offering them access to secure digital identities and financial services. Blockchain enables transparent and efficient transactions in situations where traditional banking systems are unavailable or unreliable.

The UN's interest in blockchain goes beyond humanitarian aid. It sees the technology as a way to promote sustainable development, ensure transparency in government and NGO projects, and combat corruption. By giving individuals control over their data and enabling more efficient, transparent systems, blockchain has the potential to create more equitable societies.

The Fourth Industrial Revolution: A Global Transformation
Blockchain is just one piece of the broader 4IR puzzle. The convergence of blockchain with other emerging technologies—such as artificial intelligence (AI), the Internet of Things (IoT), and augmented reality (AR)—is transforming industries across the board.

AI and Automation: Redefining Work

The WEF has long recognized the potential of AI and automation to revolutionize the workforce. While these technologies offer the potential for increased efficiency and innovation, they also pose significant challenges.

Automation could displace millions of jobs, particularly in sectors like manufacturing and retail. The WEF advocates for reskilling initiatives to prepare workers for the jobs of the future, many of which will be tied to emerging technologies like AI, blockchain, and IoT.

Blockchain and Reskilling for the Future of Work

Blockchain could play a role in this reskilling revolution by enabling decentralized education platforms. These platforms could track certifications, and as the Fourth Industrial Revolution continues to disrupt industries, the demand for new skills is skyrocketing. Blockchain has the potential to support this transition through decentralized education and credentialing systems. By using blockchain to store educational achievements and professional certifications, individuals can have a verifiable, tamper-proof record of their skills that is accessible from anywhere in the world.

This decentralized approach to education and credentials will be especially important in a world where workers need to frequently reskill and upskill to keep pace with rapidly evolving industries. Imagine a future where your academic degrees, professional certifications, and specialized skills are all stored securely on a blockchain. You'll no longer need to rely on centralized institutions or paper certificates —your skills will be recognized globally, and you'll have full ownership of your educational record.

In addition to helping individuals, blockchain-based

credentials could streamline hiring processes for companies, ensuring that candidates' qualifications are legitimate and reducing the need for lengthy background checks.

The Internet of Things (IoT): The Digital and Physical Worlds Converge

The Internet of Things (IoT) refers to the interconnected network of devices—everything from smart home appliances to industrial sensors—that communicate with each other through the internet. As IoT continues to expand, it is creating vast amounts of data and new opportunities for automation and efficiency. Blockchain plays a critical role in securing this data and ensuring that IoT systems operate efficiently.

By combining blockchain with IoT, we can create secure, decentralized networks where devices can autonomously verify transactions, communicate with one another, and take action without human intervention. For example, in smart cities, blockchain could be used to ensure that traffic lights, public transportation, and energy systems are all functioning harmoniously, securely, and efficiently.

This convergence of blockchain and IoT is foundational to the Fourth Industrial Revolution, and it's one of the key areas the WEF and other global organizations are watching closely. For investors and innovators, the intersection of blockchain and IoT presents significant opportunities, especially as industries seek ways to enhance automation and improve security.

Smart Cities and Urbanization: The Future of Urban Life

The Fourth Industrial Revolution is driving the development of smart cities, where technology is integrated into the very fabric of urban life. These cities will be powered by interconnected systems—IoT, blockchain, AI, and more—that manage everything from energy grids to public services. The goal of smart cities is to make urban life more efficient, sustainable, and equitable by leveraging technology to solve the challenges of modern urbanization.

Blockchain is expected to play a key role in enabling these smart cities. By creating transparent, decentralized networks, blockchain can facilitate everything from secure voting systems to energy trading platforms, where residents can sell excess solar energy back to the grid. Additionally, blockchain-based digital identities could allow citizens to access public services, healthcare, and financial systems more efficiently and securely.

The World Economic Forum (WEF) and other global organizations, including the United Nations and the World Bank, are actively exploring the use of blockchain to support the development of smart cities. As urbanization continues to accelerate, smart cities will become increasingly important in addressing issues such as resource management, climate change, and social inequality.

Universal Basic Income (UBI) and Digital Currencies
The automation of industries and the displacement of jobs due to the Fourth Industrial Revolution have led to growing discussions about Universal Basic Income (UBI). UBI is a policy proposal in which all citizens receive a guaranteed income to cover basic living expenses, regardless of employment status. The idea behind UBI is to ensure that people have financial security in a world where traditional employment may be less stable.

Blockchain technology could be used to implement UBI systems efficiently and transparently. By utilizing decentralized digital currencies or Central Bank Digital Currencies (CBDCs), governments could distribute UBI payments to citizens with minimal overhead costs. Additionally, blockchain would provide transparency, ensuring that funds are distributed equitably and securely.

The idea of UBI is gaining traction among global organizations like the WEF, especially as automation and AI threaten to displace millions of jobs. Whether UBI becomes a widespread reality remains to be seen, but blockchain will undoubtedly be a key technology in making such systems feasible.

Central Bank Digital Currencies (CBDCs): The Future of Money

As we move further into the digital age, Central Bank Digital Currencies (CBDCs) are becoming a major focus for global financial institutions. Unlike cryptocurrencies like Bitcoin, which are decentralized and operate independently of government control, CBDCs are digital versions of fiat currencies that are issued and regulated by central banks.

The International Monetary Fund (IMF), World Bank, and WEF have all emphasized the potential of CBDCs to modernize financial systems, reduce transaction costs, and increase financial inclusion. For countries with underdeveloped banking infrastructure, CBDCs offer a way to bring more citizens into the formal financial system, reducing poverty and improving economic stability.

CBDCs could also play a role in improving the efficiency of cross-border payments, which are currently slow, expensive, and reliant on intermediaries. With CBDCs, central banks could facilitate instant, low-cost international transfers, revolutionizing global trade and remittances.

However, the rise of CBDCs also presents challenges. Governments will have unprecedented control over citizens' financial activities, raising concerns about privacy and the potential for overreach. While CBDCs may offer efficiency and security, they also introduce new dynamics in the ongoing struggle between centralization and decentralization in the financial world.

The Club of Rome and the Global 2030 Agenda

The Club of Rome, an organization focused on global challenges such as resource depletion, climate change, and economic sustainability play a significant role in shaping global policy discussions. Like the WEF, the Club of Rome has identified blockchain and the 4IR as key to addressing these global challenges.

As part of the broader 2030 Agenda for Sustainable Development, global organizations are looking at how blockchain can help meet sustainability goals. For example, blockchain could support the efficient tracking and trading of carbon credits, ensuring that companies are held accountable for their environmental impact. Additionally, blockchain could improve transparency in supply chains, ensuring that products are sustainably sourced and that workers are treated fairly.

The 2030 Agenda aims to create a more equitable and sustainable world by addressing issues such as poverty, inequality, and climate change. Blockchain, with its ability to create transparent, decentralized systems, is seen as a key enabler of this vision.

The Great Reset: How Global Leaders View the 4IR

The concept of the "Great Reset" emerged from the WEF and other global organizations as a response to the COVID-19 pandemic. The idea is that the pandemic has accelerated existing trends—such as digitalization, automation, and inequality—and that the world must seize this moment to "reset" the global economy in a more equitable, sustainable direction.

People view blockchain and cryptocurrencies as crucial elements of this paradigm shift. By enabling decentralized finance, digital identities, and transparent governance systems, blockchain offers a way to create a more resilient and inclusive global economy.

However, the Great Reset is not without controversy. Some view it as an attempt by the global elite to consolidate power and reshape the world according to their own interests. Others see it as an opportunity to address deep-seated inequalities and build a more just and sustainable world.

The Power of Blockchain in a Changing World

Global organizations such as the WEF, IMF, WTO, UN, and others are increasingly focusing on blockchain as a key technology to navigate the challenges of the Fourth Industrial Revolution. From reshaping financial systems to creating more transparent supply chains and governance structures, blockchain is at the forefront of the global transformation.

For those of us paying attention, these developments offer an incredible opportunity to build wealth and drive positive change. By understanding the strategies of the global power elite and positioning ourselves at the intersection of blockchain and the 4IR, we can leverage this knowledge to invest in the future and become part of the new digital economy.

Several blockchain projects align closely with the 2030 Agenda for Sustainable Development, which is spearheaded by global organizations like the United Nations (UN). These projects leverage blockchain technology to promote transparency, sustainability, financial inclusion, and innovation in various sectors that contribute to the 17 Sustainable Development Goals (SDGs). Here are some key blockchain initiatives that align with the 2030 Agenda:

1. VeChain (VET): Supply Chain Transparency and Sustainability

Focus: VeChain is a blockchain platform designed to enhance transparency, traceability, and efficiency across global supply chains. By allowing businesses to track products from production to consumer, VeChain can ensure sustainable practices are followed, contributing to SDG 12 (Responsible Consumption and Production) and SDG 13 (Climate Action).

Use Case: VeChain has been applied in industries like agriculture, manufacturing, and retail to track the authenticity and sustainability of products, ensuring that they are ethically sourced and produced under environmentally friendly conditions.

2. Energy Web (EWT): Renewable Energy and Carbon Credits

Focus: Energy Web is a blockchain project focused on accelerating the transition to renewable energy and decentralized energy systems. It creates a transparent and efficient system for trading energy and carbon credits, contributing to SDG 7 (Affordable and Clean Energy) and SDG 13 (Climate Action).

Use Case: Energy Web enables peer-to-peer energy trading, where individuals and businesses can trade excess solar energy, reducing reliance on non-renewable energy sources. It also helps track carbon credits to ensure companies meet their carbon reduction commitments.

3. IOTA (MIOTA): Internet of Things (IoT) for Smart Cities

Focus: IOTA is designed to enable secure, feeless data exchange between devices in the Internet of Things (IoT) ecosystem. This project aligns with SDG 11 (Sustainable Cities and Communities) by facilitating the creation of smart cities where interconnected systems optimize energy use, reduce waste, and enhance transportation networks.

Use Case: IOTA's blockchain technology has been used in smart city projects to manage energy grids more efficiently, improve urban mobility, and promote sustainable urbanization.

4. Stellar (XLM): Financial Inclusion

Focus: Stellar's blockchain is focused on providing low-cost, cross-border payment solutions, which can help extend financial services to unbanked populations. This project directly supports SDG 1 (No Poverty) and SDG 10 (Reduced Inequality) by facilitating financial inclusion.

Use Case: Stellar enables affordable remittances, digital payments, and the issuance of stablecoins that can be used in regions with underdeveloped banking infrastructure, bringing financial services to millions of people without access to traditional banks.

5. Cardano (ADA): Sustainable Development and Governance

Focus: Cardano is known for its emphasis on sustainability, decentralized governance, and ethical solutions in blockchain technology. It aligns with multiple SDGs, including SDG 16 (Peace, Justice, and Strong Institutions) and SDG 4 (Quality Education), by focusing on building transparent, decentralized systems that empower communities.

Use Case: Cardano's blockchain is being used in projects in Africa to provide digital identities and secure land titles, offering citizens access to financial services and legal protections. It also supports education initiatives through blockchain-based credentialing and academic records.

6. Chainlink (LINK): Data Integrity and Climate Tracking

Focus: Chainlink provides decentralized oracle services that connect blockchain smart contracts with real-world data. It can be used to ensure accurate, tamper-proof data for environmental initiatives and sustainability efforts, aligning with SDG 13 (Climate Action) and SDG 15 (Life on Land).

Use Case: Chainlink oracles can verify environmental data for carbon credit markets, ensuring transparency and accountability. It is also used to track deforestation efforts and other environmental monitoring systems.

7. Tracr: Ethical Sourcing in Supply Chains

Focus: Developed by De Beers, Tracr is a blockchain platform that tracks the journey of diamonds from mine to consumer, ensuring they are ethically sourced. This supports SDG 12 (Responsible Consumption and Production) by providing consumers with transparent information about the sustainability and ethical practices behind their products.

Use Case: Tracr ensures that diamonds are conflict-free and sourced through ethical labor practices, promoting responsible consumption in the luxury goods sector.

8. Celo (CELO): Mobile-First Blockchain for Financial Inclusion

Focus: Celo is a mobile-first blockchain platform designed to bring decentralized financial services to mobile users, particularly in underserved communities. It supports SDG 1 (No Poverty) and SDG 9 (Industry, Innovation, and Infrastructure) by creating infrastructure for mobile banking and microfinance.

Use Case: Celo enables users in developing countries to access financial services via their smartphones, empowering local economies by facilitating peer-to-peer payments and access to global financial networks.

9. Food Trust by IBM: Blockchain for Food Security

Focus: IBM's Food Trust is a blockchain-based platform aimed at improving food safety, sustainability, and traceability throughout the supply chain. It aligns with SDG 2 (Zero Hunger) and SDG 12 (Responsible Consumption and Production).

Use Case: The Food Trust system allows consumers and retailers to track the journey of food from farm to table, ensuring that it is safe, sustainably produced, and free from fraud. It also reduces food waste by increasing efficiency in the supply chain.

10. Ripple Labs (XRP): Efficient Cross-Border Payments

Focus: Ripple's blockchain solutions for cross-border payments are designed to make international money transfers faster, cheaper, and more transparent. Ripple aligns with SDG 9 (Industry, Innovation, and Infrastructure) and SDG 8 (Decent Work and Economic Growth).

Use Case: Ripple's technology is being adopted by financial institutions to improve remittances and reduce the cost of cross-border payments, especially for migrant workers who send money to their families in developing countries.

11. ImpactChain: Social Impact Blockchain

Focus: ImpactChain is a blockchain platform designed to address social issues such as poverty, education, and healthcare. It supports multiple SDGs, including SDG 3 (Good Health and Well-being) and SDG 4 (Quality Education).

Use Case: ImpactChain is used to create decentralized solutions for healthcare and education, such as securely tracking patient records and delivering micro-scholarships to students in underserved regions.

12. GiveTrack: Transparency in Charitable Donations

Focus: GiveTrack is a blockchain platform developed by BitGive that allows donors to track their charitable contributions in real time. It aligns with SDG 17 (Partnerships for the Goals) by increasing transparency and trust in charitable giving.

Use Case: GiveTrack enables donors to see exactly how their funds are being used, providing transparency and accountability for charitable organizations and ensuring that contributions are used effectively.

Blockchain's Role in Achieving the 2030 Agenda

These blockchain projects align with the core goals of the 2030 Agenda by promoting transparency, sustainability, and financial inclusion. As global organizations and governments continue to adopt blockchain technology, these platforms will play a pivotal role in addressing some of the world's most pressing challenges.

Whether it's improving supply chain transparency, providing financial services to the unbanked, or enhancing the efficiency of renewable energy systems, blockchain technology is proving to be a powerful tool for driving sustainable development.

Blockchain in Healthcare: A Prescription for the Future

Blockchain is set to transform the healthcare industry in ways that will enhance security, transparency, and efficiency across the board. From ensuring the integrity of patient records to streamlining billing systems, the potential of blockchain in healthcare is vast. In this section, we'll dive into how blockchain-based projects are reshaping healthcare and how they fit into the larger vision of the Fourth Industrial Revolution.

1. Securing and Empowering Patient Records

The current healthcare system struggles with securely managing patient data, leaving it vulnerable to errors, breaches, and inefficiencies. Blockchain provides a decentralized and secure method to store patient records, giving control back to the patient while ensuring that healthcare providers have access to reliable, tamper-proof information when needed.

Blockchain-based platforms like MedRec and MedicalChain store patient data on an immutable ledger, accessible only by authorized individuals. This level of security not only safeguards sensitive information but also streamlines the transfer of medical records between providers, ensuring faster and more accurate treatment. Patients are empowered with full ownership of their data, a key shift in the digital healthcare landscape.

2. Breaking Down Barriers Between Healthcare Providers

Interoperability has long been a challenge in healthcare. Different providers often use incompatible systems, making it difficult to transfer patient information securely and efficiently. Blockchain solves this by creating a unified, decentralized network where patient records can be shared across different institutions while maintaining privacy and security.

Projects such as BurstIQ are spearheading the development of secure platforms that facilitate the sharing of health data among providers, thereby enhancing their collaboration. This reduces delays in treatment and ensures that patients receive the most informed care possible.

3. Tracking and Authenticating Pharmaceuticals

The problem of counterfeit medications and inefficient supply chains plagues the global pharmaceutical industry. Blockchain is revolutionizing the pharmaceutical industry by recording and verifying every step in the drug manufacturing and distribution process, thereby ensuring authenticity and safety.

Platforms such as Modum and MediLedger utilize blockchain to track pharmaceuticals from manufacturer to patient. This not only prevents counterfeit drugs from entering the market but also improves supply chain transparency, providing better insight into the origins and handling of medications.

4. Revolutionizing Billing and Insurance Claims

Healthcare billing systems are notoriously complex and prone to fraud. Blockchain simplifies this process with the use of smart contracts—self-executing agreements where payments are made automatically when certain conditions are met, reducing the need for intermediaries and paperwork.

Platforms like Solve.Care are already using blockchain to

streamline billing and claims processes, making payments more transparent and reducing the time needed to settle claims. This cuts down on fraud and administrative overhead, resulting in more efficient and fair healthcare systems.

5. Enhancing the Integrity of Clinical Trials and Research

The integrity of data in clinical trials is essential for the development of new treatments. Blockchain ensures that research data remains tamper-proof, increasing trust in trial results and encouraging more ethical research practices.

Blockchain platforms like PharmaLedger are revolutionizing how clinical trials are conducted by providing a transparent, secure, and immutable record of trial data. This is critical for maintaining the validity of research outcomes, ensuring compliance with regulations, and securing funding for future medical advancements.

6. Empowering Patients with Control Over Their Health Data

As patients demand more control over their healthcare, blockchain offers the ability for individuals to manage their own health records. This is a radical shift from the traditional model where medical institutions hold the data, giving patients the power to decide who can access their personal information and for what purpose.

With platforms like Patientory, patients can take control of their healthcare data, making it easier to share their medical history with providers while maintaining privacy. This patient-centric approach is a glimpse into the future of healthcare, where blockchain enables individuals to make informed decisions about their treatment.

7. Improving Medical Supply Chains

Blockchain can also be used to enhance the transparency and accountability of the medical supply chain, ensuring that products are delivered ethically and efficiently. This has become even more critical in the wake of global health crises where timely delivery of medical equipment is essential.

Platforms like Provenance use blockchain to track the journey of medical supplies, ensuring that they are sourced and delivered under ethical standards. This level of transparency helps improve trust and reliability in global healthcare systems.

Blockchain's Revolutionary Impact on Healthcare

Blockchain is more than just a technological upgrade—it's a transformative force that has the potential to overhaul every aspect of healthcare, from secure patient records to supply chain transparency. As this technology continues to evolve, its applications in healthcare will not only improve patient outcomes but will also create a more equitable, transparent, and efficient system. By embracing blockchain, healthcare providers and patients alike can participate in shaping a future where trust, privacy, and innovation are at the core of medical practice.

In the context of the 4th Industrial Revolution, blockchain stands out as a key player in the digital transformation of healthcare. By staying informed and prepared, you can position yourself to benefit from these advancements. The opportunities in this space are vast, and those who recognize the potential of blockchain in healthcare will be at the forefront of this new era.

In the previous chapter, we explored how the global power

elite, through platforms like the WEF, are shaping the future using blockchain and decentralized technologies. By following their strategies and partnerships, we begin to understand the blueprints for the 4th Industrial Revolution (4IR) and its impact on global governance and financial systems. Their focus on blockchain, digital identities, and **CBDCs**[52] indicates the wealth-building opportunities of the future.

However, there's a power struggle underway between centralization and decentralization. Governments and financial institutions are adopting blockchain not just for its efficiency but to maintain control—as seen in their development of Central Bank Digital Currencies (CBDCs) and regulatory frameworks. Meanwhile, the DeFi movement offers an alternative path: one of financial freedom, privacy, and self-sovereignty.

In the next chapter, **Centralization vs. Decentralization: The Battle for the Future of Finance** , we'll dive into this clash of ideals and explore how blockchain and the 4IR are reshaping the financial landscape. We'll look at how these competing forces will influence global economics, governance, and power. This isn't just about technology— it's about the future of wealth, freedom, and autonomy. Let's dive in.

CHAPTER 17

Centralization vs. Decentralization: The Battle for the Future of Finance

The Struggle for Control Over the Future of Money
Imagine a world where a centralized authority monitors, tracks, and controls every transaction you make. Now picture an entirely different reality, one where you have complete control over your assets, data, and financial freedom. This scenario outlines the battle currently playing out as governments and institutions push to launch Central Bank Digital Currencies (CBDCs) and tighten financial regulations while the decentralized world of cryptocurrency and DeFi pushes back. This isn't just a clash of technologies; it's a fundamental struggle over power, privacy, and personal freedom. In this chapter, we'll dive into what's truly at stake in this fight between centralization and decentralization—and why it matters more than ever.

The Battle Between Centralization and Decentralization

Two Competing Visions of the Future of Finance
At the heart of blockchain technology and cryptocurrency lies a conflict between two opposing forces: **centralization**[53] and **decentralization**[54] . This is not just a technical debate; it's a clash of ideologies. On one side,

the decentralized world offers financial systems controlled by no single entity but available to everyone. On the other hand, governments and financial institutions seek to maintain control through regulations and centralized systems like CBDCs.

Here's a breakdown of how each side envisions the future of finance.

Decentralization: Financial Freedom and Control

The Promise of a Decentralized World

Financial freedom was at the core of the original vision of cryptocurrency, particularly Bitcoin. Satoshi Nakamoto created Bitcoin as a response to the centralized control of traditional financial institutions, many of which contributed to the 2008 financial crisis. Bitcoin and the broader crypto movement offered individuals the chance to control their money without relying on middlemen like banks.

Key Principles of Decentralization:

Financial Privacy: Decentralized systems offer a degree of privacy by reducing third-party tracking and control of financial activities.

Peer-to-Peer Transactions: No need for intermediaries; users can transact directly with each other.

Censorship Resistance: Decentralized networks, like Bitcoin, are harder to shut down or control because they aren't reliant on a single authority.

Centralization: The Push for Control

The Argument for Oversight and Regulation

While decentralization offers freedom, it also comes with risks. Without oversight, it becomes easier for illicit activities like money laundering or tax evasion to occur. Governments and regulators have been grappling with how to address these risks, leading to the development of CBDCs, which offer them full control over digital currencies.

A CBDC is essentially a digital version of a country's fiat currency, controlled by its central bank. Governments see this as a way to mitigate the risks posed by decentralized cryptocurrencies while maintaining economic control.

Key Features of Centralization:

Complete Oversight: Governments can fully track CBDC transactions, enforcing regulations like KYC and AML.

Economic Control: Central banks can implement economic policies more effectively with CBDCs, including measures like negative interest rates or stimulus payments.

Security and Stability: Proponents argue that CBDCs provide a more stable and secure system compared to the often volatile crypto market.

Central Bank Digital Currencies (CBDCs): The New Frontier of Centralized Control

Why CBDCs Are Central to the Debate
Let's take a closer look at CBDCs and why they've become such a focal point in the debate between centralization and decentralization. Countries like China have made significant progress with the Digital Yuan, while nations like the U.S. and the EU are also exploring their own digital currencies.

Why CBDCs Matter:

Surveillance: CBDCs give governments unprecedented control over how money is spent. Every transaction could be tracked, allowing authorities to monitor and potentially control individual behaviors.

Monetary Policy: Unlike decentralized cryptocurrencies, CBDCs enable central banks to directly implement monetary policies like controlling inflation or issuing stimulus payments.

Financial Inclusion: Governments argue that CBDCs could help bring unbanked populations into the formal economy by providing them with access to digital financial services.

The Pushback: Defending Decentralization

The Fight for Financial Freedom
In response to this growing centralization, the crypto community continues to innovate in ways that protect financial autonomy. DeFi, **Decentralized Exchanges (DEXs)**[55], and privacy-focused cryptocurrencies like **Monero**[56] and **Zcash**[57] represent efforts to preserve decentralization.

Key Innovations Defending Decentralization:

DeFi: Decentralized finance platforms like Aave58 and Compound59 allow users to borrow, lend, and trade without the need for banks, ensuring financial autonomy.

Privacy Coins: Cryptocurrencies like Monero and Zcash focus on enhancing privacy, making it difficult for governments or third parties to trace transactions.

DEXs: Decentralized exchanges, such as Uniswap60, enable users to trade directly from their wallets without revealing their identities or complying with KYC regulations.

The future of finance might lie in a hybrid model where decentralized technologies coexist with centralized frameworks. But the question remains: how much freedom will individuals retain in managing their financial lives?

Shaping the Future of Digital Money with CBDCs?

MasterCard's Strategic Partnerships
MasterCard has positioned itself as a key player in the development of CBDCs through partnerships with **Ripple**[61], **ConsenSys**[62], and **Fireblocks**[63]. Ripple's expertise in cross-border payments offers MasterCard an advantage in enabling seamless, real-time international transactions —a critical component of any viable CBDC. ConsenSys brings Ethereum-based solutions, while Fireblocks provides institutional-grade security. Together, these partnerships provide MasterCard with a technological backbone that ensures scalability and security for digital currencies.

Ripple's XRP token plays a pivotal role in this ecosystem, with a market cap of approximately $25 billion, a current price of $0.51, and a circulating supply of 53.245 billion XRP (out of a maximum of 100 billion). Ripple's technology positions MasterCard as a leader in the evolving world of CBDCs.

These collaborations highlight more than just technological progress. They reveal MasterCard's ambition to be at the forefront of the global financial transformation as central banks increasingly explore CBDC adoption.

The Real Question: Who Will Control the Future of Money?

The Power Struggle Over the Financial System

This battle between centralization and decentralization isn't just a technical debate—it's about control. Will governments and financial institutions use CBDCs to tighten their grip on the economy, or will the decentralized movement succeed in giving individuals more autonomy over their finances?

As this debate unfolds, the rise of CBDCs marks a turning point in the future of global finance. While governments argue that these digital currencies will provide stability and inclusion, advocates of decentralization continue to push for financial freedom, privacy, and individual control. The outcome of this battle will shape the next era of economics, governance, and personal freedom.

The ongoing tension between centralization and decentralization marks a pivotal moment in the evolution of the global financial landscape. Central Bank Digital Currencies (CBDCs) offer governments a powerful means to maintain control over monetary flows, while decentralized finance (DeFi) emerges as a force for financial autonomy and individual empowerment. As we consider the future, a fundamental question arises: can these two systems coexist in harmony, or will one ultimately overshadow the other?

In the next chapter, we'll delve into the **Basel III Endgame**[64] a strategic initiative designed to fortify global financial systems against future economic shocks. As we explore Basel III's vision of resilience, we'll also see how emerging technologies like **ISO 20022**[65] and certain cryptocurrencies aim to support this goal, creating a more robust financial infrastructure. Together, these innovations promise to play pivotal roles in shaping a more stable, interconnected, and resilient global financial system.

CHAPTER 18

The Global Reach of Banking Regulations and the Rise of ISO 20022

The Silent Revolution in Finance

When we think of global finance, images of towering skyscrapers, bustling trading floors, and influential central banks may come to mind. Yet, beneath these symbols of financial power lies a less visible but equally transformative layer—international standards that enable smooth, secure transactions across the world. One such standard, ISO 20022, is reshaping financial systems globally. By establishing a universal "language" for financial messaging, ISO 20022 is transforming transaction speed, transparency, and security, quietly initiating a revolution in how financial institutions connect and communicate.

As ISO 20022 takes hold, select cryptocurrencies—like Ripple, **Stellar, and Quant**[67] —are aligning with this standard to position themselves as more than digital assets. These cryptos are becoming integral to the evolving financial ecosystem, setting the stage for a future in which they help drive efficient, secure cross-border payments on a global scale. In this chapter, we'll explore the far-reaching effects of new banking regulations, examining how ISO 20022 and the strategic *Basel III Endgame* work in concert to create a more resilient financial system—and why these shifts matter for the future of digital finance.

Banking Regulations: A Global Framework

Building a More Resilient Financial System

Banking regulations are the backbone of a global financial framework that extends beyond individual economies, shaping and stabilizing the financial systems of interconnected nations. The 2008 financial crisis underscored the need for stronger, coordinated international regulations, prompting initiatives like the Basel III Endgame, which requires banks to hold more capital and better manage risk. This approach aims to fortify financial institutions against crises and prevent another global collapse.

Creating a resilient, interconnected system demands that central banks, financial institutions, and regulators coordinate efforts, ensuring seamless communication across borders. Here, ISO 20022 takes center stage, designed to standardize international transaction messaging and foster an efficient, secure global financial system. Through ISO 20022 and Basel III, the groundwork is laid for a more resilient future, paving the way for cryptos and digital assets to play a significant role in a new, fortified financial order.

Introduction to ISO 20022 and SWIFT Migration

The New Standard for Global Financial Messaging

ISO 20022 is the future of global financial messaging. Developed by the International Organization for Standardization (ISO), this standard aims to replace outdated **SWIFT**[68] messaging systems. It enables financial institutions to communicate using a universal format rich in data and adaptable for future technologies like blockchain and digital currencies.

As SWIFT migrates to ISO 20022 (a transition expected to be completed by 2025), cross-border payments will become faster, more transparent, and more secure. This migration isn't just a technical upgrade—it's a fundamental shift in how money moves worldwide.

The Benefits of ISO 20022

Why It's a Game-Changer
ISO 20022 is set to revolutionize financial transactions. Here's why:

- **Rich Data Formats:** Supports detailed and structured data, minimizing errors and ensuring smoother transactions.
- **Enhanced Interoperability:** Improves the ability of institutions to process payments across borders using a universal standard.
- **Increased Efficiency:** Enables faster, cheaper transfers, benefiting businesses and individuals alike.
- **Future-Proof Design:** Built to evolve with emerging technologies like blockchain, ensuring smoother integration with digital currencies and decentralized finance.

Cryptocurrencies Aligning with ISO 20022

The Future of Finance

Certain cryptocurrencies are positioning themselves for mass adoption by aligning with ISO 20022. These digital assets are structured not just for peer-to-peer transactions but to integrate seamlessly into the traditional financial system. Here are some of the major players:

1. Ripple (XRP)
Use Case: Cross-border payments and remittances.

Adoption Potential: With partnerships spanning major financial institutions, Ripple is a leader in the cross-border payment space.

Market Cap: $25 billion.

Key Feature: Ripple's On-Demand Liquidity (ODL) system leverages XRP for fast, efficient cross-border transactions.

2. Stellar (XLM)
Use Case: Payments, with a focus on financial inclusion.

Adoption Potential: Partnerships with companies like **IBM** suggest Stellar's potential for serving underserved markets.

Market Cap: $7 billion.

Key Feature: Stellar's low-cost, rapid transfers are ideal for unbanked populations.

3. Quant (QNT)
Use Case: Bridging traditional finance and blockchain.

Adoption Potential: Quant's Overledger technology allows interoperability between different blockchain networks.

Market Cap: $1 billion.

Key Feature: Quant's focus on connecting blockchains to traditional systems is crucial for the future of decentralized finance.

4. Algorand (ALGO)[69]

Use Case: DeFi, smart contracts, cross-border payments.

Adoption Potential: Algorand's scalability makes it a key player in future financial applications.

Market Cap: $1.5 billion.

Key Feature: Pure Proof-of-Stake (PPoS) ensures fast, efficient transactions with minimal energy use.

The Impact of ISO 20022-Compliant Cryptocurrencies

Bridging Traditional and Decentralized Finance

As institutions worldwide adopt ISO 20022, compliant cryptocurrencies stand to gain widespread acceptance. These assets could serve as the bridge between DeFi and traditional banking systems, making them pivotal players in the evolving financial ecosystem.

ISO 20022 is more than a technical update—it's the foundation for a future where blockchain-based assets, DeFi, and traditional finance coexist in a more transparent, efficient global economy. This is part of a broader transformation linked directly to the Fourth Industrial Revolution, where digital, physical, and biological systems merge, creating new opportunities for those who understand and act on these shifts.

The rise of ISO 20022 highlights a significant shift toward integrating traditional finance with decentralized technologies. Cryptocurrencies that align with this standard are positioning themselves as essential components of the new global financial system. But the story doesn't end here. As we explore the internet's evolution—from Web 1.0 to Web 3.0—we'll see how blockchain, cryptocurrencies, and decentralized networks are reshaping not just finance but society as a whole.

In the next chapter, we'll delve into **The Evolution of the Web: From Web 1.0 to Web 3.0 and Beyond.** We'll explore how the internet's transformation mirrors the broader changes in finance, offering a roadmap for leveraging these developments to secure wealth, influence, and digital autonomy in the age of decentralized power.

CHAPTER 19

The Evolution of the Web: From Web 1.0 to Web 3.0 and Beyond

Decentralizing the Web: The Promise of Web 3.0
Picture yourself in the early days of the internet. Websites were static, just blocks of plain text with little to no interaction. You were a passive observer, scrolling through content but not really engaging. Now fast forward to today—an era where the internet buzzes with life, from streaming videos and shopping online to social media interactions and decentralized apps (dApps) running on blockchain. The internet has transformed from its humble beginnings into something much more dynamic. But what's next? **Web 3.0**[70] promises a future where power is decentralized, data belongs to the users, and the internet becomes a place where you control your digital identity and assets.

The First Web: Web 1.0: The Static Era
When the internet first started to gain popularity in the early '90s, it was far from the vibrant, interconnected world we see today. **Web 1.0**[71], also known as the "Static Web," laid the groundwork for modern communication, but let's face it—it was nothing like the digital playground we have now.

Read-Only Information: Web 1.0 was a one-way street. Although users could read and consume content, they could only interact by clicking links and browsing static pages.

Limited User Interaction: There was no chance to create content—users were just consumers. A few content creators or companies would push information to passive users.

Centralized Control : Large organizations or governments hosted these early websites, leading to a highly centralized structure where users had little power.

Web 1.0, although foundational, was limited, and users were mere spectators in the digital world. The web needed to evolve—and evolve it did with **Web 2.0[72]**.

The Interactive Web: Web 2.0: The Social Revolution
Web 2.0, the "Social Web," took things to a whole new level, adding interaction and dynamism to the internet. Suddenly, you weren't just consuming content—you were creating it. This was a complete game-changer.

- **User-Generated Content:** Platforms like YouTube, Facebook, and Twitter handed the power of creation to the users. You could post thoughts, share videos, and contribute to global conversations.

- **Real-Time Interaction:** The web became live and interactive. Comments, likes, and shares happened in real-time, creating an always-on environment.

- **Centralized Data Control:** However, this

came with a catch. As social platforms
grew, so did their control over user data.
Tech giants like Google, Facebook, and
Amazon became the gatekeepers of user
data, raising concerns about privacy and
monopolization.

While Web 2.0 revolutionized how we communicate and
connect, it also brought about issues of centralized control.
Users gained interactivity but lost ownership over their
data, setting the stage for Web 3.0.

The Decentralized Web: Web 3.0—The Internet Reimagined

Enter Web 3.0—an internet powered by decentralization,
blockchain technology, and user sovereignty. If Web 2.0
gave us interactivity, Internet 3.0 promises empowerment.
Built on blockchain and distributed networks, Web 3.0
provides the tools for users to control their data, privacy,
and online presence. Here's how Web 3.0 is reshaping the
digital landscape:

- **Decentralization:** Web 3.0 moves
  away from centralized servers owned by
  corporations and governments. Instead,
  data is spread across decentralized
  networks, making it much harder for any
  one entity to control.

- **Blockchain and Smart Contracts:**
  Blockchain lies at the heart of Web
  3.0, allowing for peer-to-peer interactions
  without intermediaries. Smart contracts
  execute transactions based on pre-
  programmed rules, removing the need to
  trust third parties.

- **User Ownership:** The core philosophy of Web 3.0 is user sovereignty. Users own their data, digital assets, and even their online identities through decentralized solutions like blockchain-based IDs.

- **Tokenization**[73]: Everything from currency to art and real estate can be tokenized and traded on blockchain platforms. Web 3.0 is creating entire online ecosystems of value, including Decentralized Finance (DeFi) and Non-Fungible Tokens (NFTs).

- **Interoperability**[74]: Web 3.0 aims to seamlessly connect everything—people, devices, applications, and networks—through interoperable protocols, without centralized control.

Web 3.0 isn't just the next phase of the internet; it's a shift in how we think about digital ownership, privacy, and interaction.

How Blockchain Powers Web 3.0
Blockchain technology is the engine driving Web 3.0. Without it, decentralization wouldn't be possible. Here's how blockchain shapes this new internet:

- **Decentralized Finance (DeFi):** Web 3.0's DeFi platforms allow users to borrow, lend, and trade without needing banks or brokers. DeFi cuts out the middleman, democratizing access to financial services.

- **Decentralized Storage:** Platforms like **Filecoin** or **IPFS** store data across decentralized networks, giving users ownership of their data without relying on traditional cloud services like Amazon Web Services.

- **Decentralized Autonomous Organizations (DAOs):** DAOs use blockchain to create transparent organizations that are governed by smart contracts and token holders.

The Potential Impact of Web 3.0

The transition to Web 3.0 will upend industries and redefine how we interact online. Here's how this new era could reshape our world:

- **Finance:** Decentralized exchanges and tokenized assets could transform traditional finance, making it more inclusive and efficient.

- **Healthcare:** Blockchain could secure health records, ensuring privacy and controlled access to sensitive information.

- **Supply Chain Management:** Blockchain's transparency ensures full traceability, reducing fraud and verifying product authenticity.

- **Digital Identity:** Web 3.0 will enable people to control their digital identities, eliminating reliance on centralized ID verification systems like passports.

- **Governance:** DAOs will make governance more transparent and democratic, enabling communities to vote on key issues and have decisions executed via smart contracts.

Did You Know?

Astar, Chainlink, and Polkadot Powering Japan's Web3 Future
Japan's Web3 ecosystem is rapidly evolving, and the partnerships between **Astar**[75], **Chainlink**[76], and **Polkadot**[77] are leading the charge. Astar Network, which supports decentralized applications, has aligned with Chainlink to offer decentralized oracles, providing secure, real-time data for smart contracts. Polkadot, on the other hand, facilitates interoperability, allowing blockchains to communicate and function seamlessly together. These partnerships are critical to Japan's Web3 development, ensuring scalable, secure, and efficient decentralized applications.

As of now, Astar (ASTR) holds a market cap of $218 million, priced at $0.054, with an all-time high of $0.33. Chainlink (LINK), a key player in Web3, boasts a market cap of $7.7 billion, a price of $8.20, and an all-time high of $52.88, with 538 million LINK in circulation. Meanwhile, Polkadot (DOT) has a market cap of $5.4 billion, priced at $4.38, with an all-time high of $55.

This trio of blockchain technologies—Astar for dApps, Chainlink for data, and Polkadot for interoperability—forms the backbone of Japan's emerging Web3 infrastructure. Their collaboration illustrates how blockchain is not only advancing innovation but also real-world applications, driving forward the broader context of the 4th Industrial Revolution.

CHAPTER 20

The Metaverse: Blending Physical, Digital, and Virtual Worlds

Beyond Reality: Understanding the Metaverse
We've explored how blockchain, the Internet of Things (IoT), and decentralized infrastructures are reshaping our world, but what if these technologies didn't just enhance our current reality? What if they created an entirely new one—a world where the boundaries between physical and digital are so blurred it's hard to tell where one ends and the other begins? A space where imagination meets technology, only limited by creativity.

Welcome to the **Metaverse**[78], a vast, immersive digital universe merging virtual and physical realities, where interactions, economies, and experiences are as tangible as the lives we lead. In this chapter, we'll step into this new realm where blockchain evolves beyond decentralized finance and digital identities to become the architecture of entire worlds—worlds that are built, owned, and governed by their inhabitants.

We'll dive into the concept of the Metaverse, the role of **AR**[79], **VR**[80], **MR**[81], and **XR**[82] technologies in creating this immersive space, and how blockchain and Web 3.0 redefine ownership, interaction, and existence in this new digital frontier.

From Science Fiction to Everyday Reality

In 1992, **Neal Stephenson**[83] introduced the world to the concept of the Metaverse in his novel Snow Crash, a virtual space where people could escape the limitations of their physical reality. What seemed like far-off fiction is now becoming our reality. Blockchain technology, in tandem with advanced virtual and augmented reality isn't just creating new digital spaces—it's building the infrastructure of entirely new worlds. The Metaverse is evolving, moving from sci-fi pages to something you can step into, interact with, and build upon.

What is the Metaverse?

At its core, the Metaverse is an interconnected digital universe—a blend of multiple virtual worlds, augmented spaces, and immersive experiences where users can interact with one another and their surroundings in ways previously reserved for the physical world. Unlike today's internet, where we passively view content, the Metaverse is a fully immersive space where we don't just watch but live within the content.

Key Characteristics of the Metaverse:

- **Persistence:** The Metaverse never pauses or stops. Just like a city that never sleeps, it continues to evolve whether you're logged in or not, filled with constant activity driven by its users.

- **Interoperability:** Unlike fragmented platforms, the Metaverse allows seamless movement between different worlds and experiences. Your avatar, digital assets, and identity remain consistent and recognized across the Metaverse.

- **Decentralization:** Powered by blockchain, the Metaverse rejects centralized control. Users own their data, assets, and identities, managing them through decentralized networks without the need for intermediaries.

- **User-Created Economies:** The Metaverse thrives on user-generated content and economies. Virtual land, avatars, in-game assets, and digital creations are bought, sold, and traded on blockchain-powered markets, turning virtual value into real-world assets.

- **Immersion:** Through AR, VR, MR, and XR technologies, the Metaverse is a fully immersive experience. It's not just a place to observe but to live in, interact with, and shape.

AR, VR, MR, and XR: The Gateways to the Metaverse

The door to the Metaverse is opened through immersive technologies like AR, VR, MR, and XR, each offering unique ways to blend the physical and digital worlds.

- **Augmented Reality (AR):** Enhances your physical environment by overlaying digital content on top of it. AR will let you interact with digital objects while navigating your real-world space.

- **Virtual Reality (VR):** Fully immerses you in a digital world. With a VR headset, you're transported into entirely new environments, whether it's a virtual concert or an alien landscape.

- **Mixed Reality (MR):** Blends digital and

physical objects, making them interact in real-time, allowing you to manipulate digital elements within your real environment as if they were tangible.

- **Extended Reality (XR):** The umbrella term for AR, VR, and MR, offering a spectrum of immersive experiences that transport users deeper into the Metaverse.

The Metaverse and Web 3.0: A New Digital Frontier

The Metaverse represents the digital home of Web 3.0, the next evolution of the internet. While Web 2.0 centralized control among tech giants, Web 3.0—powered by blockchain—returns control to the users. This decentralized web aligns perfectly with the Metaverse's principles of ownership, privacy, and autonomy.

Decentralized Identity and Ownership:

Web 3.0 grants users full control over their digital identities and assets. In the Metaverse, your avatar, virtual property, or even your business belongs entirely to you—not a central authority.

Interoperability through NFTs:

Non-Fungible Tokens (NFTs) ensure your assets are portable across different worlds. You can take your avatar from one digital concert to a gaming session in another virtual space, with NFTs ensuring authenticity and ownership.

Smart Contracts for Seamless Transactions:

In the Metaverse, smart contracts automate everything from virtual real estate purchases to event ticketing. No middlemen are needed—just code that executes transactions based on predefined conditions.

Decentralized Economies and DAOs:
Decentralized Autonomous Organizations (DAOs) allow users to collectively build and govern digital worlds, offering new models of virtual governance.

Reimagining Daily Life in the Metaverse
The Metaverse isn't just a gaming hub or a virtual escape —it's a space poised to reshape everyday life, business, and social interaction:

- **Virtual Workspaces:** Work in a digital office with colleagues from around the world, interacting as avatars in 3D spaces.

- **Digital Real Estate:** Just as in the physical world, virtual land is bought, sold, and developed, creating a new frontier for real estate investment.

- **Education:** Imagine learning in immersive virtual environments, walking through ancient Rome, or exploring the human body from the inside out.

- **Entertainment and Social Interaction:** Attend concerts, festivals, and gatherings from anywhere in the world, all within the Metaverse.

The Metaverse as Our Next Reality
The Metaverse isn't just a digital experiment—it's the future of how we live, work, and socialize. Its decentralized structure, powered by blockchain, will fundamentally change our understanding of ownership, identity, and community. As AR, VR, and Web 3.0 technologies continue to grow, they will blend our digital and physical realities in unprecedented ways.

This convergence leads us to a critical question: How

will society continue to evolve as the world becomes increasingly digitized? The answer lies in recognizing that the future is not only virtual or digital but also deeply integrated with human progress. The Metaverse is just the beginning.

In this last chapter, we explored the Metaverse as a transformative space where the physical, digital, and virtual worlds converge. This shift aligns with the goals of the 4th Industrial Revolution (4IR), a movement recognized by organizations like the World Economic Forum (WEF), which forecasts a future where global economies and digital ecosystems are deeply interconnected. By embracing these technologies, societies and investors alike can tap into new opportunities and innovations that redefine traditional industries and markets.

The next chapter **The NFT Revolution: Owning the Digital World** delves into how gaming—long considered a form of entertainment—is evolving into a digital economy powered by blockchain and NFTs. We'll explore how these technologies reshape the gaming industry, creating new ways for players to earn, own, and trade digital assets, ultimately redefining the way we interact with games and digital worlds. Join us as we uncover the future of gaming in the era of decentralization, where play and profit intersect.

CHAPTER 21

The NFT Revolution: Owning the Digital World

From Collectibles to Crypto: My Introduction to NFTs

Back when I was a kid, I collected things like baseball cards and comic books. Owning these physical items gave me a sense of pride, and I could trade or sell them if I wanted to. Today, that same sense of ownership has moved to the digital realm, thanks to Non-Fungible Tokens (NFTs). Originally starting with digital art and collectibles, NFTs have evolved into something much bigger, reshaping industries from gaming to real estate. When I first encountered NFTs, I was intrigued but skeptical—how could something digital be owned? After all, the internet is a place where everything can be easily copied. But as I delved into the technology behind them, I realized that NFTs represent a paradigm shift in ownership, especially within the 4th Industrial Revolution.

NFTs: The Building Blocks of Digital Ownership

A blockchain records an NFT as a unique digital asset. Unlike cryptocurrencies like Bitcoin or Ethereum, which are fungible and interchangeable, each NFT is unique. Blockchain technology backs this uniqueness, ensuring that each NFT is provably authentic and owned by a single individual or entity.

Before NFTs, digital goods like music or art were infinitely replicable. However, NFTs introduce digital scarcity, offering a new frontier for collectors, artists, and gamers by embedding ownership and value into the code itself. Whether it's a piece of digital art, a song, or virtual real estate, NFTs give creators unprecedented control over their work and allow consumers to verify their ownership, providing proof of authenticity and value.

From Art to Everything: NFTs' Expanding Reach

NFTs may have first gained attention in the world of digital art, but their applications have expanded to include music, real estate, and even sports. Notable artists like Beeple broke records when an NFT art collage sold for $69 million at Christie's, demonstrating the enormous potential for digital ownership.

In the music industry, artists are using NFTs to interact directly with fans. Kings of Leon, for example, became one of the first bands to release an album as an NFT, offering exclusive perks like limited-edition vinyl and VIP concert access. Similarly, the real estate industry is exploring virtual land sales using NFTs on platforms like Decentraland and The Sandbox, allowing users to own, trade, and develop digital property.

Gaming and NFTs: Power to the Players

The gaming industry has arguably seen the most transformative impact from NFTs. In traditional gaming ecosystems, like those on PlayStation or Xbox, players purchase in-game items that they never truly own. These purchases are locked within the game, and once the game shuts down, the items are lost.

With NFTs, this changes. Blockchain technology ensures that in-game assets are unique and tradable across platforms. Players can now truly own their digital assets, whether it's a rare weapon, avatar skin, or character.

This new form of digital ownership has shifted the power dynamics within the gaming industry, and major companies like Sony and Microsoft are already recognizing the potential. Both companies have filed patents to integrate NFTs into their gaming ecosystems, potentially allowing players to sell, trade, or transfer their in-game assets across multiple games or even sell them in open marketplaces.

This shift explains why the gaming industry now generates more revenue than the combined music, film, and TV industries. Gamers are willing to pay for unique digital assets, and NFTs provide the mechanism for true ownership.

NFTs and Web3: Building a Decentralized Internet
NFTs play a pivotal role in the wider transition to Web3, a decentralized internet platform based on blockchain technology. Unlike Web2, where centralized platforms like Facebook and Google dominate, Web3 empowers users to control their data, digital identities, and assets.

In this decentralized ecosystem, NFTs act as proof of ownership. Whether you're purchasing digital land, attending virtual concerts, or owning in-game assets, NFTs offer verifiable ownership and transferability across decentralized platforms. As Web3 continues to develop, NFTs will serve as the building blocks of this new, user-owned internet.

The Pros and Cons of NFTs in the 4th Industrial Revolution
As NFTs reshape industries, they bring both benefits and challenges.

Pros:

- **True Ownership:** NFTs enable users to have full control over their digital assets, allowing them to buy, sell, and trade freely.

- **Empowering Creators:** Artists, musicians, and game developers can monetize their work directly without relying on traditional gatekeepers.

- **Interoperability:** Users have greater flexibility across digital ecosystems when they can transfer NFTs between different platforms.

- **Scarcity:** By embedding scarcity into digital goods, NFTs create value in a way that was impossible in the past.

Cons:

- **Environmental Impact:** NFTs often rely on energy-intensive blockchains like Ethereum, raising concerns about their carbon footprint.

- **Market Volatility:** The NFT market is highly speculative, with values fluctuating wildly depending on market trends and demand.

- **Legal and Regulatory Hurdles:** The legal landscape for NFTs is still evolving, and issues around intellectual property rights and ownership are a growing concern.

- **Barrier to Entry:** Creating and selling NFTs can be expensive due to high gas fees on certain blockchains, limiting access to wealthier individuals.

The Role of NFTs in the 4th Industrial Revolution
As we move further into the 4th Industrial Revolution, NFTs will play a critical role in shaping how we interact with the digital and physical worlds. In a world increasingly connected by the Internet of Things (IoT) and AI, NFTs will be at the center of emerging economic models, digital identities, and decentralized systems.

Imagine a future where your car, home, or even medical records are tied to NFTs, giving you full control over access and ownership. This future isn't far off. NFTs and blockchain are already paving the way for new solutions in digital rights management, helping ensure creators are fairly compensated for their work, especially in the age of AI-generated content.

The future of NFTs is far more expansive than what we see today. NFTs have the potential to transform not only digital art and gaming, but also finance, real estate, and even government. NFTs could serve as collateral for loans or integrate into investment portfolios as DeFi (Decentralized Finance) expands. Governments and corporations are also exploring how NFTs can be used in supply chain management to track and verify goods, enhancing transparency and trust.

Closing Thoughts: NFTs as the Building Blocks of the 4IR
The journey from gaming's early days to the blockchain-powered, decentralized gaming ecosystems of today highlights how technology evolves alongside human creativity. Gaming has grown beyond simple entertainment; it's become an economy, a marketplace, and a community. By integrating blockchain, NFTs, and decentralized models, the industry is pioneering new

forms of ownership, participation, and monetization, setting the stage for how digital economies will function within the 4th Industrial Revolution (4IR).

As we transition into the final chapter, it's important to see how the themes of decentralization, smart cities, digital ownership through NFTs, and IoT, each explored in the preceding chapters, converge. They form the building blocks of this new era. This isn't just about evolving technology; it's about reshaping human progress.

In this 4IR, connectivity, automation, and decentralization come together to create a new landscape, one where individuals have more control and communities are empowered to reshape their own economies.

In the final chapter, **"The 4th Industrial Revolution: A New Dawn of Human Progress,"** we'll bring everything full circle. We'll explore how these technological advancements are not just influencing individual industries but are becoming the foundation for a new socio-economic paradigm. It's a new dawn, where the innovations of the past chapters merge, offering unprecedented opportunities for those prepared to adapt, invest, and lead in this rapidly changing world.

CHAPTER 22

The 4th Industrial Revolution: A New Dawn of Human Progress

The 4th Industrial Revolution: Redefining Innovation and Industry

We've journeyed through the intricacies of blockchain technology, cryptocurrencies, decentralized finance (DeFi), Web 3.0, the Internet of Things (IoT), smart cities, and the boundless potential of the Metaverse. Each of these innovations represents a transformative shift in how we experience and interact with the world. But these are not isolated breakthroughs; they are interconnected pieces of a much larger puzzle, a revolution so all-encompassing that it has been coined by Klaus Schwab, the founder of the World Economic Forum (WEF), as the 4th Industrial Revolution (4IR).

This revolution is a fusion of advancements in artificial intelligence (AI), machine learning, blockchain, IoT, robotics, quantum computing, and other cutting-edge technologies. In this era, the lines between the physical, digital, and biological worlds are blurring, driving unprecedented change across industries and society itself. It's not just about new technologies, it's about redefining human progress.

In this final chapter, we'll revisit the core ideas we've

covered, exploring how they come together in the 4th Industrial Revolution. We'll conclude by asking the critical question: Do we truly understand the magnitude of the changes happening? And more importantly, how can we position ourselves to thrive in this new era?

More Than Just a Technological Leap

The 1st Industrial Revolution brought mechanization through steam power. The 2nd introduced electricity, fueling mass production and global trade. The 3rd, the digital revolution, connected the world through computers and the internet. But the 4th Industrial Revolution is something entirely different. It's not just about machines, it's about the merger of technology with humanity itself. The future is no longer just smart; it's intelligent, interconnected, and autonomous. From AI to blockchain, we are evolving with the very technology we create.

The Journey Through Technological Transformation

As we stand on the precipice of the 4th Industrial Revolution, it's essential to reflect on how we arrived here. Every technology we've discussed is a building block of this new world:

- **Blockchain Technology and Bitcoin:** We started by exploring how blockchain, the foundational technology behind Bitcoin, introduced the idea of decentralized, transparent, and secure digital systems. This decentralized ledger redefined what was possible in finance, making it the backbone of the crypto revolution.

- **Ethereum and the Rise of Altcoins:** Ethereum took blockchain a step further, introducing smart contracts and decentralized applications (dApps), sparking the era of altcoins and opening up endless possibilities beyond Bitcoin's original scope.

- **Technological Infrastructure of Cryptocurrencies:** The infrastructure behind cryptocurrencies, exchanges, cross-chain tools, and interoperability became essential as the ecosystem expanded. Alongside this growth, governments responded with regulatory frameworks aimed at balancing decentralization with compliance.

- **Stablecoins and Meme Tokens:** The duality of the crypto market emerged: stablecoins provided stability, while meme tokens, though often volatile, highlighted the community-driven and speculative side of this emerging economy.

- **Malfeasance in the Crypto Industry:** With innovation came exploitation. From scams to frauds, the dark side of the crypto industry reared its head. This emphasized the need for caution and governance to navigate a space where the stakes are high.

- **World Economic Forum and the Vision for Blockchain:** The WEF provided us with a macro lens, showing how blockchain is part of a broader 4IR vision, one that is shaping everything from economies to societies.

- **Centralization vs. Decentralization:** The tension between government oversight and the decentralized ideals of blockchain became a theme throughout, with regulations like KYC and AML reflecting this ongoing battle between control and freedom.

- **Fintech as a Guardrail Against Economic Collapse:** The integration of blockchain into fintech has the potential to prevent future economic crises, with decentralized systems offering transparency, stability, and resilience in ways traditional finance never could.

- **Web Evolution and IoT:** The web has evolved, from the static nature of Web 1.0 to the interactive Web 2.0 and now to Web 3.0, decentralized, secure, and user-owned. Simultaneously, the IoT is weaving a web of interconnected devices, leading us toward smarter systems.

- **Smart Cities and the Metaverse:** We examined how smart cities, powered by IoT and blockchain, and the Metaverse, with its immersive experiences, are converging to create a new blend of digital and physical existence.

- **IoT and Interoperability:** The promise of blockchain-enhanced IoT is a world where devices can communicate autonomously, creating a future that operates seamlessly across systems.

- **The Metaverse and Web 3.0:** Finally, we explored the Metaverse, an interconnected digital universe where our digital identities, assets, and communities thrive, all supported by Web 3.0 principles.

The Culmination of Technological Convergence in the 4th Industrial Revolution

The 4th Industrial Revolution is not just a continuation

of the digital revolution but a full-scale convergence of multiple technologies, each of which is transformative in its own right. Together, they are reshaping industries and human life in profound ways.

Here are the key dimensions of this revolution:

- **Artificial Intelligence and Machine Learning:** AI is at the core of 4IR, enabling machines to learn, adapt, and improve autonomously. From personal healthcare to automated financial systems, AI is driving innovation in every corner of society.

- **Blockchain and Decentralization:** As the foundation of the decentralized economy, blockchain provides the infrastructure for secure, transparent, and trustless systems. In the 4th Industrial Revolution, blockchain will be essential for managing decentralized identity, digital assets, and automated systems.

- **Quantum Computing:** With its potential to solve problems beyond the reach of classical computers, quantum computing could unlock new advancements in cryptography, drug discovery, and artificial intelligence, pushing the boundaries of what is possible.

- **IoT and Real-Time Decision Making:** IoT is creating a network of interconnected devices that generate and share data in real time. Combined with blockchain, IoT will lead to smarter cities, homes, and industries, optimizing efficiency and creating unprecedented transparency.

- **Extended Realities (XR):** Augmented, virtual, and mixed realities are transforming how we experience the world. These technologies are foundational to the Metaverse, enabling fully immersive, interactive digital environments that are blurring the boundaries between the virtual and physical worlds.

- **Ethics, Privacy, and Cybersecurity:** As we advance, protecting personal data and ensuring cybersecurity will be more crucial than ever. Blockchain will play a central role in safeguarding our digital lives and ensuring trust in a world where data is the new currency.

As this revolution unfolds, the responsibility lies with us —to ensure that the technologies of tomorrow are used to empower individuals, promote equity, and address the challenges facing our world. We stand on the cusp of this monumental shift and face a critical question: How will you position yourself in the 4th Industrial Revolution? The technologies we've explored—blockchain, cryptocurrencies, DeFi, smart cities, AI, and the Metaverse —are not just future concepts. They are the foundation of the new world we're building, a world where opportunity exists for those who are willing to take action now.

But here's the truth: as of today, very few retail investors in the USA and globally are involved in these transformative industries. Recent statistics show that while over 21 million Americans own some form of cryptocurrency, this is still a small fraction of the population, and the percentage of active participants in the blockchain ecosystem is even smaller. Globally, the situation is the same. Less than 5% of the world's population is actively investing in these cutting-edge areas, meaning 95% of people are missing out on the incredible opportunities this new era presents.

The Time to Invest is Now

There has never been a more critical time to get involved. The cryptocurrency market is expanding, and altcoins are creating new avenues for growth. Initial Coin Offerings (ICOs) are allowing early investors to get in on the ground floor of revolutionary projects. And it doesn't stop there. From stablecoins that offer financial stability to speculative meme tokens that tap into cultural movements, there's an endless array of opportunities in the crypto space.

Beyond crypto, the entire ecosystem of the 4th Industrial Revolution offers unique investment possibilities. Whether you're interested in gaming, NFTs, or the Metaverse, the potential to build wealth is limitless. The emergence of Decentralized Finance (DeFi) platforms is already disrupting traditional finance by creating open, transparent financial systems that anyone can access. And with the rise of Web3, individuals are gaining control over their data and assets in ways we've never seen before.

Sectors Poised for Explosive Growth

The following sectors are ripe for explosive growth if you're looking to invest in this new age:

- **Blockchain:** The backbone of decentralized systems, with applications in everything from finance to healthcare.

- **Cryptocurrencies and Altcoins:** Digital currencies offering alternatives to traditional banking and fiat currency.

- **Stablecoins:** Assets pegged to real-world

currencies, providing stability in a volatile market.

- **Initial Coin Offerings (ICOs):** Early-stage investment opportunities in new blockchain projects.

- **NFTs (Non-Fungible Tokens):** digital ownership of unique assets, reshaping industries like art, music, and real estate.

- **The Metaverse:** A virtual universe where digital identities and economies thrive, creating limitless possibilities for investment.

- **DeFi (Decentralized Finance):** An open financial system built on blockchain, allowing users to lend, borrow, and trade without intermediaries.

- **Web3:** The next iteration of the internet, where individuals own and control their digital identities and data.

- **Smart Cities:** Cities powered by IoT and blockchain, optimizing urban life through technology.

- **IoT (Internet of Things):** A network of interconnected devices revolutionizing industries from healthcare to agriculture.

- **Fintech:** The fusion of technology with finance, streamlining payments, lending, and banking services.

- **AI (Artificial Intelligence):** Driving automation and intelligence in nearly every industry.

- **MR, XR, VR, AR:** Mixed, extended, virtual, and augmented realities are reshaping how we experience the world, with investment opportunities ranging from gaming to healthcare.

Building Generational Wealth in the 4th Industrial Revolution

As we stand at the edge of the 4th Industrial Revolution, we're witnessing changes that are unlike anything humanity has ever experienced before. The technological advancements we've explored in this book —blockchain, AI, IoT, the Metaverse, decentralized finance —are not just transforming industries but reshaping everyday life itself. From the way we bank, shop, work, and even communicate, these technologies are fundamentally altering the fabric of society. The question now is: **Are you ready?**

This revolution is both an opportunity and a challenge. While it offers endless possibilities for those who are prepared, it also presents massive disruptions, especially in the job market. The very nature of work is changing, and millions of jobs that exist today may soon vanish. The middle class, the backbone of many societies, is at risk, and the lines between the wealthy and the less fortunate are being redrawn. In this chapter, we'll explore the winners and losers of this new era and discuss how you can ensure you're on the winning side.

CHAPTER 23

A New Reality: Technology's Impact on Everyday Life

Technology and Transformation in the Modern World
The technologies driving the 4th Industrial Revolution are already reshaping how we live. Here's a look at some of the most significant changes:

- **Transportation:** Autonomous vehicles (AVs) are already on our roads, with companies like Tesla, Uber, and Google racing to perfect self-driving technology. Soon, truck drivers, rideshare drivers, and delivery personnel could see their jobs taken over by AVs and drones.

- **Retail and Warehousing:** Amazon and other retailers are using robots and AI to manage inventory, package delivery, and customer service. The need for human workers in warehouses, fulfillment centers, and service roles will continue to diminish as automation advances.

- **Manufacturing and Production:** Factories worldwide are becoming highly automated, with AI-driven machines producing goods faster and more efficiently than ever. This shift is eliminating millions of jobs in manufacturing sectors globally.

- **Service Industry:** Jobs like receptionists, call center workers, and customer service agents are increasingly replaced by AI chatbots and virtual assistants. Tasks once requiring a human touch are now managed by automated systems operating 24/7.

- **Healthcare:** Even in the healthcare industry, where human expertise is invaluable, AI diagnostic tools, robotic surgery assistants, and telemedicine platforms are reducing the need for human intervention in routine tasks and consultations.

These examples illustrate how technology is already transforming the job market. As we move deeper into the 4th Industrial Revolution, these changes will accelerate, and jobs across industries will either evolve or disappear entirely. *Will you be a victim of these changes, or will you seize the opportunity to thrive in this new era?*

The Jobs Crisis: What the Numbers Tell Us

The shift toward automation and AI is expected to result in significant job losses. According to a report from the World Economic Forum, 85 million jobs could be displaced by automation and AI by the end of 2025. In the U.S. alone, it's projected that one-third of all jobs will be replaced by automation within the next decade. Truck drivers, warehouse workers, customer service representatives, and even professionals in fields like finance and medicine are not immune to these changes.

At the same time, the 4th Industrial Revolution will create new job opportunities in fields such as data science, blockchain development, cybersecurity, and AI programming. However, these positions will require specialized skills. The middle class, which has traditionally relied on stable, well-paying jobs, is particularly vulnerable. The wealth gap is expected to widen dramatically as low-skill jobs disappear, leaving millions without the skills necessary to compete in the new economy.

Choose Your Future: Be a Victor, Not a Victim
This is the reality of the 4th Industrial Revolution: **Millions of jobs will be lost**, and many more will require new skills. The wealth gap will widen further, and those who don't adapt face the risk of falling behind. But here's the positive news: **You don't have to be a victim.** By taking action now, you can secure your future and thrive in this new era.

Investing in blockchain technology, cryptocurrencies, and other innovations emerging from the 4th Industrial Revolution is one of the smartest moves you can make. These technologies aren't just disrupting industries— they're creating entirely new ones. From decentralized finance (DeFi) to smart cities, Web3, and the Metaverse, the potential for growth is endless.

- **Blockchain** will redefine how businesses and governments operate.
- **AI** will drive innovation across healthcare, finance, and education.
- **IoT** will connect devices and systems, creating smarter cities and homes.
- **Web3** will usher in a new internet where users have more control over their data and assets.

The opportunities to invest and participate in these technologies are abundant, from cryptocurrencies and

NFTs to smart contracts and DeFi platforms. The question is: **Are you ready to act?**

Call to Action: Your Role in the 4th Industrial Revolution

We are living through one of the most transformative periods in human history, and you have the power to decide where you stand. The future will be shaped by those who take action—those who invest in new technologies and embrace the potential of blockchain, AI, and the 4th Industrial Revolution.

It's time to get involved. Whether you're investing in cryptocurrencies, exploring opportunities in DeFi, or positioning yourself for the future by learning about blockchain and smart contracts, the opportunities for generational wealth are there. Join me in the **Bigger Than Bitcoin Course,** where you'll gain the tools and knowledge needed to thrive in this new world. And don't stop there—become part of the **Bigger Than Bitcoin Community,** a network of like-minded people working together to build wealth and success in the 4th Industrial Revolution.

Timing is Everything: The Future is Yours to Shape

You have two options: stand still and watch as the 4th Industrial Revolution leaves you behind, or control your future by learning, investing, and becoming part of the revolution. The window of opportunity is closing quickly, and those who act now will be the ones who build lasting wealth and prosperity in the coming decades.

The choice is yours: Will you be a victim or a victor in the 4th Industrial Revolution?

Endnotes

1. **Bitcoin:** the first cryptocurrency, introduced the concept of decentralized digital currency, which operates without the need for a central authority or intermediary.
2. **Blockchain:** is the underlying technology behind Bitcoin, a distributed ledger system that ensures transparency, security, and immutability in digital transactions.
3. **Bitcoin ATMs:** allow users to buy and sell Bitcoin using cash or other forms of payment, making cryptocurrency more accessible to the general public.
4. **Sell limit order:** allows investors to automatically sell a stock or cryptocurrency when it reaches a specific price, in this case, $20,000 for Bitcoin.
5. **Bid-ask spread:** represents the difference between the price buyers are willing to pay and the price sellers are asking for an asset, like Bitcoin.
6. **CBD (Cannabidiol):** is a compound found in cannabis that is often used for medicinal purposes, becoming a growing industry in recent years.
7. **The crypto space:** refers to the global ecosystem of blockchain technology, cryptocurrencies, and the communities that support and develop them.
8. **Altcoins:** refer to alternative cryptocurrencies to Bitcoin, each with varying use cases, utilities, and blockchain technologies.
9. **Dogecoin, Ethereum, Litecoin,** and **XRP:** are examples of well-known altcoins with distinct features and blockchain networks.
10. **Data ownership:** refers to individuals' control over their personal information and the ability to decide how it is shared and used, a principle enabled by blockchain's decentralized structure.

11. **The Great Reset:** is a proposal by the World Economic Forum to reshape economies and societies in response to global crises, with blockchain often seen as a tool for this transformation.

12. **Digital wallets:** are tools for storing and managing digital assets and currencies, enabling faster and more secure transactions.

13. **Satoshi Nakamoto:** the pseudonymous creator of Bitcoin, whose true identity remains unknown.

14. **DeFi (Decentralized Finance):** refers to a system of financial services built on blockchain technology that operates without traditional intermediaries like banks or brokers.

15. **Ledgers:** Record-keeping systems used to document financial transactions.

16. **Double-Spending:** The risk that digital currency could be spent more than once in traditional systems without central oversight.

17. **Solana is a blockchain** known for its speed and scalability, with a growing ecosystem of decentralized applications.

18. **Hedera (HBAR):** A decentralized public network designed for fast, secure, and scalable enterprise applications.

19. **4th Industrial Revolution:** The ongoing transformation driven by advanced digital technologies like AI, blockchain, and IoT.

20. **Web3:** refers to the next generation of the internet, where blockchain technology empowers users with more autonomy over their data and digital transactions.

21. **IoT (Internet of Things):** connects everyday devices to the internet, allowing seamless data exchange and interaction, with blockchain playing a key role in enhancing its security and

trust.

22. **Hot Wallet:** A digital wallet connected to the internet, used for everyday transactions.
23. **Cold Wallet:** An offline wallet used for secure, long-term storage of digital assets.
24. **NFTs (Non-Fungible Tokens)** are unique digital assets stored on the blockchain, representing ownership of items like digital art, collectibles, and virtual real estate, offering verifiable proof of ownership and scarcity.
25. **Shoebox:** A metaphor for a safe place to store physical currency, often in the home.
26. **Public Key:** A cryptographic key that allows users to receive cryptocurrency and is freely shareable.
27. **Private Key:** A cryptographic key used to authorize transactions and control digital assets must be kept secret.
28. **KYC (Know Your Customer):** A regulatory requirement for financial institutions to verify the identity of their customers.
29. **AML (Anti-Money Laundering):** A set of regulations to prevent money laundering through financial systems.
30. **PayPal:** An online payment system that supports online money transfers.
31. **Ledger:** A company known for its hardware wallets used in cryptocurrency storage.
32. **Ethereum:** is a decentralized blockchain platform that enables smart contracts and decentralized applications (dApps).
33. **Stablecoin:** A cryptocurrency designed to maintain a stable value, often pegged to fiat currencies.
34. **Meme Token:** A cryptocurrency driven primarily by community sentiment, often without intrinsic value or use cases.

35. **Dogecoin:** A meme-based cryptocurrency that gained popularity through social media and internet culture.

36. **Shiba Inu:** A cryptocurrency inspired by Dogecoin, known for its strong community following.

37. **Tether (USDT):** A widely used stablecoin backed by reserves of fiat currency.

38. **USD Coin (USDC):** A stablecoin known for its transparency and regular audits.

39. **Dai (DAI):** A decentralized, crypto-collateralized stablecoin governed by MakerDAO.

40. **Tether Market Cap:** The market value of all USDT tokens in circulation.

41. **USD Coin Market Cap:** The market value of all USDC tokens in circulation.

42. **Binance USD Market Cap:** The market value of all BUSD tokens in circulation.

43. **Dai Market Cap:** The market value of all DAI tokens in circulation.

44. **MakerDAO:** A decentralized organization that governs the DAI stablecoin.

45. **TrueUSD Market Cap:** The market value of all TUSD tokens in circulation.

46. **Dogecoin Market Cap:** The market value of all DOGE tokens in circulation.

47. **Shiba Inu Market Cap:** The market value of all SHIB tokens in circulation.

48. **Pepe Market Cap:** The market value of all PEPE tokens in circulation.

49. **Floki Inu Market Cap:** The market value of all FLOKI tokens in circulation.

50. **Baby DogeCoin Market Cap:** The market value of all BabyDoge tokens in circulation.

51. **DAOs (Decentralized Autonomous Organizations):** are blockchain-based entities

governed by smart contracts and community votes, allowing for decentralized decision-making without a traditional central authority.

52. **CBDCs (Central Bank Digital Currencies):** are government-issued digital currencies designed to provide a digital form of fiat money, offering the advantages of cryptocurrency while maintaining central control through national banks.

53. **Centralization:** The concentration of control and decision-making authority in a single governing body or authority.

54. **Decentralization:** Shifts control and decision-making across distributed networks, often utilizing blockchain technology to promote transparency, autonomy, and security.

55. **Decentralized Exchanges (DEXs):** operates without a central authority, allowing peer-to-peer trading of cryptocurrencies directly from users' wallets, offering increased privacy, reduced reliance on intermediaries, and greater control over funds compared to traditional centralized exchanges.

56. **Monero:** A privacy-focused cryptocurrency that uses advanced cryptographic techniques, such as ring signatures and stealth addresses, to ensure that transactions are untraceable and confidential, distinguishing itself as one of the most secure and private digital assets available.

57. **Zcash:** Another privacy-centric cryptocurrency that offers users the option of "shielded" transactions, which use zero-knowledge proofs to enable fully private transactions, while still allowing for public verifiable transactions when desired.

58. **Aave:** Is an open-source decentralized finance

(DeFi) protocol that enables users to lend and borrow cryptocurrencies without relying on a centralized intermediary.

59. **Compound:** Is a decentralized finance (DeFi) protocol that enables users to lend and borrow cryptocurrencies.

60. **Uniswap:** A decentralized exchange (DEX) protocol built on the Ethereum blockchain that facilitates the automated trading of cryptocurrencies through smart contracts.

61. **Ripple:** Is widely known for its role in facilitating cross-border payments using blockchain technology. By leveraging its XRP Ledger, Ripple enables fast, efficient, and low-cost international transactions, particularly aiming to modernize the traditional banking and remittance sectors.

62. **ConsenSys:** An Ethereum-based blockchain software company, plays a critical role in developing infrastructure for Central Bank Digital Currencies (CBDCs). Through its expertise in decentralized finance (DeFi) and smart contracts, ConsenSys aims to help countries launch programmable money and expand financial inclusion.

63. **Fireblocks:** A digital asset security platform that provides institutional-grade custody, asset management, and secure transfer services for cryptocurrencies and digital assets. Its secure infrastructure makes it a crucial partner in the development and management of CBDC systems.

64. **Basel III Endgame:** A global regulatory framework developed by the Basel Committee on Banking Supervision.

65. **ISO 20022:** A global standard for electronic data interchange between financial institutions, facilitating structured and efficient

communication across financial systems.

66. **Stellar (XLM):** A decentralized protocol designed for fast, low-cost cross-border payments.

67. **Quant (QNT):** Focuses on solving the challenge of blockchain interoperability through its Overledger technology.

68. **SWIFT:** Is migrating to ISO 20022 to improve cross-border payments by 2025, a shift that enhances financial communication.

69. **Algorand:** Has a PPoS system that allows for quick, low-energy transactions ideal for DeFi applications.

70. **Web 3.0:** Promises user sovereignty, placing data ownership back into the hands of individuals.

71. **Web 1.0:** Refers to the static era of the internet, where content was primarily consumed rather than created by users.

72. **Web 2.0:** Brought interactivity and user-generated content to the forefront, revolutionizing the way we engage online.

73. **Tokenization:** On blockchain platforms creates digital ecosystems where assets like currency, art, and real estate can be traded.

74. **Interoperability:** Web 3.0 connects people, devices, and applications seamlessly across decentralized networks.

75. **Astar Network:** A multi-chain decentralized application (dApp) platform built on the Polkadot ecosystem.

76. **Chainlink:** A decentralized oracle network that enables smart contracts on various blockchains to securely interact with real-world data, APIs, and traditional financial systems.

77. **Polkadot:** A next-generation blockchain protocol designed to enable multiple blockchains to operate seamlessly together, achieving

interoperability and scalability.

78. **Metaverse:** Combines virtual worlds, augmented realities, and immersive experiences, blending physical and digital spaces.

79. **Augmented Reality (AR):** Integrates digital content into the physical world, allowing users to interact with virtual objects while navigating real-world environments.

80. **Virtual Reality (VR):** Immerses users in entirely digital environments, creating experiences that transport them beyond the physical world.

81. **Mixed Reality (MR):** Enables the interaction of digital objects and physical environments in real-time, creating a blended reality.

82. **Extended Reality (XR):** Serves as the overarching term for AR, VR, and MR technologies, offering various levels of immersive experiences.

83. **Neal Stephenson:** Wrote a novel *Snow Crash* is widely credited with popularizing the concept of the Metaverse.

EPILOGUE

Your Journey Is Just Beginning Thank you for joining us on this journey through the Fourth Industrial Revolution and the transformative power of cryptocurrency and blockchain. As you take these insights further, remember that "It's Still Not Too Late to Be Early." The knowledge you've gained here is just the beginning of an expansive world that's reshaping our future.

To keep your momentum going, visit us at www.biggerthanbitcoin.io and www.theurbancrypto.io. Here, you'll find additional resources, insightful articles, and the latest trends in blockchain, crypto, and decentralized technology. Dive deeper with the Bigger Than Bitcoin community, and let's build the future together.

Stay connected with us on social media, where we share daily updates, industry insights, and exclusive content to help you stay ahead. Remember, we say, " Yes to E.I.S.— Educate, Inform, and Strategize." Let's educate ourselves, inform one another, and strategize collectively to create wealth and drive positive change.

If you're ready to keep growing, learning, and shaping the future, come join our community, connect with like-minded pioneers, and explore the many tools we have to offer. Because, ultimately, "If Not You, Then Who?" Together, we can build a future that's "Bigger Than Bitcoin."

ACKNOWLEDGEMENT

Writing this book has been a transformative journey, and it would not have been possible without the unwavering support, guidance, and belief of so many people who have stood by me through every challenge and victory.

I am first and foremost grateful to my entire family. I owe a great deal to both of my children, your trust, belief, and love saved my life. Your curiosity and even mistakes opened doors that have changed our lives forever. Watching you embrace your life journey inspires me. You are the foundation of my resilience and my determination to keep moving forward, no matter the odds.

To my parents for their unwavering support and belief in me. I will always wish I could take the pain away. Your belief in me, even when the path seemed uncertain, has been a beacon of strength and perseverance. I am who I am because of the values you instilled in me.

To my siblings, who never gave up on me even in my darkest moments. Your faith in my vision, your loyalty, and your belief in what I was building kept me going when I thought about giving up. Thank you for holding me accountable, for pushing me to stay the course, and for being there when I needed you most.

To my battle buddies both in the military and on the streets—thank you for standing by my side in the trenches, whether on the battlefield or navigating the complexities of life. The lessons we learned together, the brotherhood we formed, and the grit we developed have shaped me in ways words cannot express.

To my friends and business partners who helped me find my voice, fine-tune my vision, and build a platform for everyone. It's our shared commitment to give everyone the chance to benefit from the massive changes that are transforming the world, and I am honored to have journeyed alongside you.

To the cryptocurrency and blockchain community, thank you for embracing innovation and daring to push the boundaries of what's possible. Your passion for decentralization and building a better future for all continues to inspire me. I'm grateful for the knowledge shared, the challenges faced, and the progress made. This book is not just a reflection of my efforts but a testament to the communities, friendships, and alliances that have helped shape my journey. I'll always be grateful for your light, love, and belief that anything is possible.

ABOUT THE AUTHOR

Dan "Worldwide" Worthy

Dan "Worldwide" Worthy, a Brooklyn native and crypto Technology educator, leverages his street smarts, military training, and academic achievements to showcase the power of blockchain technology. After a troubled youth marked by felony charges, homelessness, and surviving the violent streets of New York City, Worthy obtained his GED at 16. Redirected from Riker's Island to Army Basic Training at 19, he embraced the discipline that transformed his life.

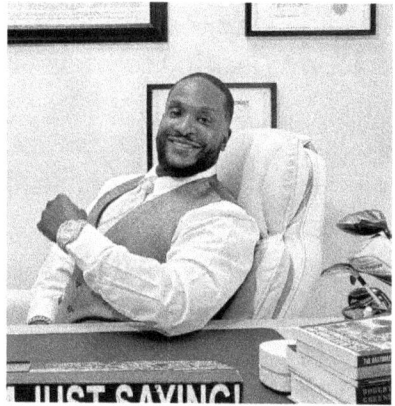

After serving and deploying during Operation Enduring Freedom, Dan transitioned from military to civilian life by pursuing education. He earned an associate degree from Monroe Community College, followed by a bachelor's and double master's from Rochester Institute of Technology. These achievements led to a successful corporate career, where Dan rose to senior leadership positions at BWI

Airport, managing one of the largest state contracts and overseeing hundreds of staff.

Dan's drive for knowledge led him into entrepreneurship, where he launched several ventures, learning valuable lessons from each experience. In 2017, Dan Worthy became "Worldwide" Worthy after a six-figure cryptocurrency cash-out allowed him to fulfill his dream of world travel. This success fueled his passion for educating others on the transformative power of crypto technology. His insights, shared on social media, quickly gained traction, leading to widespread requests for advice.

Today, Worthy is continuing his journey as a crypto pioneer, deeply engaged in the community, and focused on the educational empowerment of everyday people. Worthy's journey is a unique blend of street survival, military discipline, academic success, entrepreneurial spirit, and forward thinking. His story serves as an inspiration for those overcoming obstacles, demonstrating that hard work, diverse skills, and determination can shape a brighter future.

www.ingramcontent.com/pod-product-compliance
Lightning Source LLC
Chambersburg PA
CBHW061327220326
41599CB00026B/5065